BASIC ILLUSTRATED

Freshwater Fishing

Edited by FalconGuides

FALCONGUIDES

GUILFORD, CONNECTICUT
HELENA, MONTANA
AN IMPRINT OF GLOBE PEQUOT PRESS

FALCONGUIDES®

FalconGuides is an imprint of Globe Pequot Press.
Falcon, FalconGuides, and Outfit Your Mind are registered trademarks of Morris Book Publishing, LLC.

Project editor: Julie Marsh, Staci Zacharski
Layout: Mary Ballachino

Library of Congress Cataloging-in-Publication data is available on file.
ISBN 978-0-7627-9266-5

Printed in the United States of America
10 9 8 7 6 5 4 3 2 1

Contents

CHAPTER ONE

Before You Go

Choosing Your Fishing Style

The first question you need to ask yourself is: Am I baitfishing, spincasting, or fly fishing? Each style has its virtues, strengths, and rewards. Don't listen when an angler tries to argue that one method of fishing is inherently superior to another. They're preaching on behalf of a style that works for *them*; it doesn't mean it's necessarily going to work for you.

Are you a true beginner, and just want to go catch a fish? Is there a bass pond out the back door that looks inviting? Baitfishing might be the way to go. Do you want to introduce your children to fishing without having them become overly frustrated by the experience? Again, baitfishing might be the best choice.

Later, having caught a few fish and wanting more control over how you fish a particular piece of water, you should perhaps take a look at spincasting. You can target particular species and sizes, make more controlled casts, and find the satisfaction that comes from matching exactly the right lure with exactly the right fish.

Later still, having caught a satisfying number of fish and having

SHUTTERSTOCK / STEVE BRIGMAN; FACING PAGE: SHUTTERSTOCK/MICHAEL G. MILL

spent enough time on the water that you've become intrigued by the habitat and the food sources, fly fishing offers an entirely new portfolio of challenges. For most fly fishers, catching fish is almost incidental to the acquisition of various skill sets. Having presented yourself with certain challenges (learning new casts, tying new flies, etc.), catching a nice fish becomes evidence of success, not necessarily success in itself.

Having made your first, crucial decision, you can then proceed to making more informed choices regarding rods and reels, baits, and lures. Everything follows from these first choices.

Before setting out to the store, here are some questions to consider:

> Have I ever fished before?
> Will I be keeping the fish I catch?
> Am I fishing with children? Inexperienced adults?
> Am I fishing in moving water or in still water?
> Will I be using a guide to help me along?

In making your choice, think as well about the places you'll want to fish and the type of fish you anticipate catching.

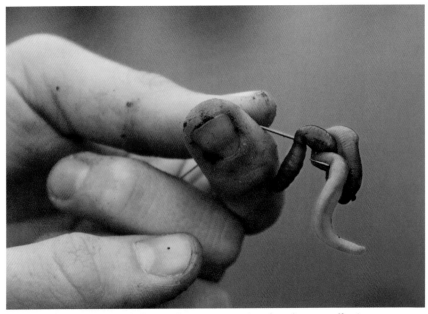

The most traditional bait of all—earthworms—is quite often the most effective.
SHUTTERSTOCK / JPS

Baitfishing

Criteria

For those just getting started with fishing, baitfishing provides (arguably) the easiest way to begin spending time on the water. And certainly for kids, baitfishing makes for a smoother introduction. A Styrofoam cup full of night crawlers, a cheap rod and reel from your corner sporting goods store, a hook and a bobber, and a backyard pond . . . next thing you know, you're fishing.

While baitfishing is more dependable in terms of potential action (fish will hit a worm or minnow long after they've rejected every other lure), there is a trade-off. Baitfishing tends to be a bit harder on the fish. Fish will have a greater tendency to swallow a hook with a worm on it than an equivalent hook dangling below a spoon. So if you're planning on releasing your catch, it's a good idea, at the very least, to flatten the barbs on your hooks or even consider transitioning to a spinning outfit. If a fish does swallow the hook and you still want to release it, the common wisdom maintains that it's better to cut the line and leave the hook in the fish's belly. Chances are good that the metal will rust loose without further harming the fish.

Baitfishing also tends to be a bit more suited to still-water fishing than moving water.

Rods and Reels

Baitcasting reels of various sizes should be matched with an appropriate rod to create a balanced outfit. Most baitcasting reels range from 6 to 9 ounces in weight but can differ in line capacity, gearing, and number of ball bearings. With many quality models, you can choose combinations of weight, line

A pistol-grip rod works well for one-handed casting. BRUCE CURTIS

capacity, gearing, and cranking power. The varying sizes of
conventional reels also depend
on their application and differ
mainly in their line capacity and
gearing.

> **Women's Gear**
>
> In the early years of gear innova-
> tion, it was impossible for women to
> find rods that easily fit their hands
> or waders that were tailored to their
> forms. Thankfully, the fishing industry
> has woken up and now provides, in
> almost every category, gear that is
> targeted specifically toward women.

Just about any kind of
line works with most baitcasting reels—monofilament and
superbraids or other superlines.
This gives the angler a significant range of performance,
depending upon the kinds of lures or rigs being used. Most conventional reels
are loaded with monofilament line. Some baitcasters also have quick-remove
spools, in case you need to switch quickly from monofilament to braided line.
Braided line is ideal for heavier-duty applications, such as when you're fishing
from boats and using bottom rigs for big fish.

When it comes to rods, the target fish species and lure selection often
dictate the length and action of a baitcasting rod. Most baitcasting rods
range from 5½ feet to 7½ feet, depending upon the casting distance and fish-
fighting strength you need. The bigger the fish, the bigger the rod you should
use. Rods with a trigger grip underneath the reel seat and short handle are
designed specifically for one-handed casting.

Spincasting
Criteria
You've been around fishing a bit, and you're interested in taking it to the next
level: exploring different lures, matching different styles of casting with different water types and scenarios. From your time with baitfishing, you have
a feel for an appropriate casting motion. Based on your time on the water,
you're also a bit more conservation-minded, interested in releasing more fish
than you keep. It's time to move to a spinning outfit.

Rods and Reels
There are two types of reels to be concerned with here: spincast and spinning reels. Both are highly popular, due mainly to their ease of use and great
applicability. You can use either one for just about any species of freshwater
fish and for nearly every kind of freshwater lure and fish-catching tactic. Spincast reels sit atop the rod and require smaller line guides, while spinning reels
hang below the rod handle and call for much wider guides.

A standard spinning reel has a turning bail and a line roller that wraps line around a central spool. BRUCE CURTIS

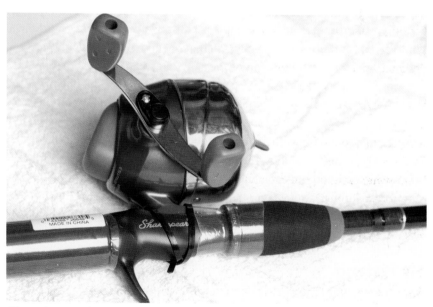

Most spincast reels are meant for freshwater fishing, and thus don't have excessively strong drags or high line capacity. BRUCE CURTIS

Spincast reels are usually the best starter reels for kids, as they are easily understood and operated—just push the line-release button and cast. Such reels are most often paired with line from 4-pound test up to 12-pound test and work best when matched to a lure or sinker that weighs from ⅛ to ¼ ounce.

The best light and ultralight reels are often spinning reels, designed for very light rods, lines, and lures. Larger freshwater spinning reels can be easily matched to 15- or 20-pound test and can cast lures or sinkers weighing up to 1½ ounces.

On a spinning reel, the turning bail and line roller wraps line around a central spool; the spool moves in and out on a shaft as the bail turns so line is wound uniformly. To cast, flip the bail open and catch the line with a finger, holding it taut, then release it at the end of the cast. The drag-adjustment knob is usually atop the spool or at the back of the reel.

Most spincast reels don't have excessively strong drags or high line capacity. Nearly all come with an anti-reverse mechanism, which keeps the spool from turning backwards during casting. With the first turn of the crank after a cast, the spool-release button snaps back into place, ready for the next cast. To match most spincasting reels, you won't need a rod that is much over 6 feet long; for kids, a 5- to 5½-foot rod is plenty. As for spinning rods, most of them range from 5½ to 7 feet long, depending on application.

As you expand your spinning and spincasting endeavors and go after different kinds of fish, you're going to learn more and more about how rod and reel selection matter in terms of strategy. Can you succeed with a limited number of rods and reels? Yes, if you match the tackle to the fish and are willing to use a variety of lines and rigs. Let's say you actively pursue farm-pond bass and big-river catfish, and sometimes trout in mountain creeks. That calls for three different basic outfits: ultralight or very light (trout), medium-light (bass), and medium to slightly heavy (catfish). If you load some stronger line on that bass rod, you can easily use it for the catfish, though it might not have as much backbone as you may want for casting heavier sinkers or beating big fish. And you could also get away with putting some heavier line on the trout rod and using it as your backup bass rod.

Fly Fishing
Criteria
As your experience with fish and fishing habitats grows, you may wish to experiment with other tackles, other methods. You may wish to create new goals for yourself, learn new casting and retrieval techniques, and study the local insect hatches and nymph types. You may even want to imitate the food sources of your quarry by tying your own flies. Fly fishing, which predates

There is nothing quite like landing a fish that took a fly that you tied yourself.

spinning and spincasting by roughly a century, delivers a virtually weightless fly to a fish by using a weighted line and a rod that rolls out that line. Most people think immediately of trout when they think of fly fishing—and that's sensible, as the origins of fly fishing are found in the effort to cast imitations of various insects to feeding trout—but nowadays people fly fish for everything from smallmouth bass to sailfish.

Rods and Reels

Fly reels hold line and put drag on running fish, and don't do much else. They have pretty simple mechanical systems. They're made of polycarbonate, lightweight alloys, and aluminum. Under the line itself, the reel is loaded with "backing," a thin-diameter line that fills the reel and backs up the 60- to 80-foot fly line.

The fly rod is the more crucial piece of tackle. Fly rods are classified according to weight and by various levels of "action," or flexibility: slow, or full flex; medium, or mid-flex; and fast, or tip-flex (the stiffest). In general, the slower models are lighter rods used for smaller species, mid-flex rods are used for a variety of medium to large species, and tip-flex rods are used for long casts with heavier lines for larger fish.

When people speak of a 7-weight rod or a 9-weight rod, they're actually talking about the line weight the rod is designed to carry. The line-weight

While most fly reels have a simple drag system, the reel is important primarily as a way of holding line. The far more important piece of equipment is the rod. DAVID DIRKS

The backing is tied between the fly line and reel. In this case, the backing is a slightly darker stack of line nearest to the center of the reel. DAVID DIRKS

system, from 0 to 12, is the basis of the tackle and relates to the actual weight of the line in "grains." Lighter lines, and thus smaller reels, range from 0 to 4; medium lines range from 5 to 7, with reels slightly larger. The heaviest lines for the largest species range from 8 to 12. Most fly rods are a tube of graphite from 7 to 9 feet long, and come in two- to five-piece models. For short casts on small water, a 7-foot fly rod is all that's needed; longer casts on bigger water call for 9- or 10-foot rods.

Fly Lines

Figuring out what line to use with which reel and rod is where fly fishing
befuddles a lot of anglers. There are so many different configurations of fly
line, and the crucial properties of rods differ widely size by size and from
maker to maker.

Most anglers start with a mid-weight fly rod, usually a 5- or 6-weight,
with moderate flexibility (medium action). Fly casters usually use a "weight-
forward" (WF) line—a line that has a larger diameter at the forward end, which
makes that end heavier than the rest of the line. This weight carries the line
using the force the rod gives it during a cast. Depending upon application, a

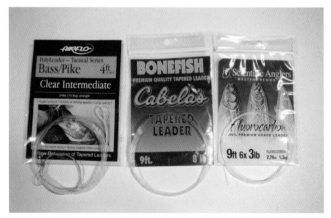

*A leader is tied between the fly line and the fly. Leaders come in
a variety of styles, lengths, and weights, and should be chosen
according to the fish you're targeting that day.* DAVID DIRKS

fly line floats or sinks, slowly or quickly. A weight-forward, floating line for a 6-weight outfit is abbreviated "WF6F," whereas a sinking line of the same size is "WF6S."

Rod choice connects to line performance. Casting a light, 3-weight floating line to small-stream trout calls for a quite flexible (slow-action) 3-weight rod. Casting a 9-weight sinking line on a big river requires some power, and for that you would select a 9- or 10-weight mid-flex or tip-flex (fast-action) rod, depending on your casting ability and style.

Leaders and Tippets

The leader is the clear piece of monofilament or fluorocarbon that attaches to the end of the line. A leader's length, strength, and diameter are very particular, given that you might be casting a small fly that must be tied to a very light "tippet"—the terminal section of the leader—but might be fishing for big trout that can really fight, so you need a leader of some strength. Freshwater fly leaders are also quite a bit longer than usual, anywhere from 7 to 12 feet.

You can make leaders by connecting lighter and lighter sections of monofilament with blood knots (see page 93), or you can buy premade tapered one-piece leaders that get thinner and thinner down to the last 30 inches or so, which is the tippet section.

Freshwater fly leaders are classified by their tippet size, usually from 0 to 6; the higher the number, the thinner the diameter. Tippets also have an "X" suffix: 1X, 2X, 3X, etc. The X is a holdover from the days when leaders were passed through a razor-sharp tool to make the tippet thinner and thinner; for

As opposed to leaders, which are typically tapered and come in a variety of lengths, tippet material is a consistent weight throughout and comes in a spool. Tie a tippet on the end of your leader and replace it during the course of your day. DAVID DIRKS

example, a 4X leader passed through the tool four times. Tapered monofilament leaders are now created chemically. For floating flies, especially for wary trout, a longer leader of about 9 or 10 feet is necessary, possibly longer. When casting big flies to tough freshwater species, such as big largemouth bass, a short, strong tippet works best.

Fly Essentials

Just like any other fishing, fly fishing is about the right presentation of the correct lure. While there are applications, such as casting poppers to largemouth bass or streamer flies to trout, that can be easily matched with conventional lures cast from spinning or baitcasting outfits, there are some things that only a fly caster can do, such as hook trout that are entirely focused on mayflies.

Bass poppers can be cast with either a fly rod or a spinning outfit. SHUTTERSTOCK / DAS-FOTO

By and large, flies can be divided into three groups: surface flies (including dry flies and attractors such as bass poppers); streamers (typically meant to imitate baitfish, leeches, crustaceans, etc.); and nymphs (often meant to imitate the nymphal stage of emerging insects, such as mayflies; just as often, however, "nymph" is a generic term referring to underwater food sources such as scuds or freshwater shrimp).

Smart anglers also take along all the effective tackle they might need, and many switch between fly rods and spinning or baitcasting rods as conditions change, fish move, and different challenges arise.

COMPLETING YOUR OUTFIT

After buying your rod and reel, line, and lures, make your day on the water as comfortable and successful as possible by investing in some other items as well. Consider a set of waders (hip or chest), a tackle box or vest, hemostats for removing hooks from fish, clippers for trimming line, and polarized sunglasses to better see fish underwater. Make a checklist before you go to the store. And don't forget the sunscreen and bug dope!

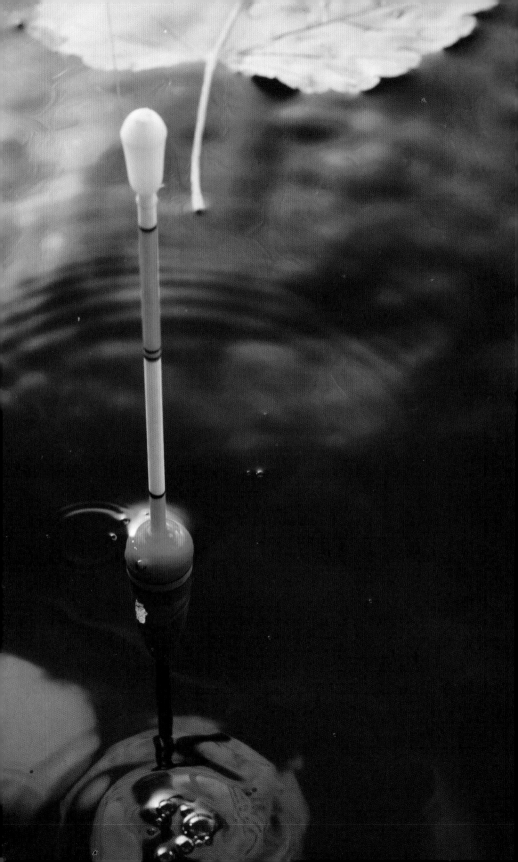

CHAPTER TWO

Baitfishing Basics

When the uninitiated think of fishing, they may think of a lazy afternoon on the banks of a warm pond, bare feet and a bee buzzing past, a simple rod and reel and a red-and-white bobber. And while there's something to be said for this passive, sit-and-wait approach to baitfishing, it turns out that there's quite a lot more to baitfishing than this image would imply. Indeed, from the choice of hooks to the style of casting and picking the right bait, there is a deceptive science to the sport.

Hardware

Baitcasting Reels

Reels with a horizontal, rotating spool that releases line at a right angle predate spinning and spincasting reels by many years. Such reels and those used for fly casting were the two main types of reels in America for much of the late nineteenth century and first half of the twentieth century. The tricky casting of these old conventional reels—which often suffered tangles of overrun, unspooled line, called "backlash"—led many anglers to take up spinning and spincasting gear.

But state-of-the-art baitcasting and conventional reels are now widely used in America, with baitcasting reels taking a lead role in professional bass fishing. They have

As you cast with a baitcasting reel, the outflow of line from the spool is regulated by your thumb. DAVID DIRKS; FACING PAGE: SHUTTERSTOCK / MIKHAIL HOBOTON POPOV

better cranking power than spinning or spincasting gear and can thus handle some serious fish. They are also quite accurate for casting.

To cast a baitcaster, depress the spool-release clutch with the thumb of your casting hand. As you depress the clutch, slide your thumb forward so it presses against the spool, securing the spool so it won't turn. Depressing the clutch creates "freespool"—the gears are disengaged and the spool can release line very easily. Use thumb pressure to control the spinning of the spool as you make your cast.

Lines and Leaders

A look at any fishing-gear retail catalog reveals a confusing array of fishing lines. How do you figure out what you need? That depends on the type of fishing you're doing, the type of reel that you use, and what you want to spend.

Monofilament continues to be the most popular fishing line. You can use it most anywhere for anything, and it consistently works very well with all kinds of fishing reels. In general, monofilament (nylon) tends to be the least expensive line. After that, there are fluorocarbon lines. This kind of line has extremely low visibility in water—some manufacturers will say it's invisible. If you fish very clear water, or for very spooky wild fish, it might be a key choice.

Then there are the "superlines"—braided lines that are fused or spun together using very thin synthetic fibers. These very small-diameter lines offer strength equal to or greater than their monofilament counterparts. They also tend to be more expensive than monofilament.

Both monofilament and fluorocarbon come in a variety of low-visibility colors. Each line type has its strengths and weaknesses. BRUCE CURTIS

Apart from being much stronger than simple monofilament line, braided lines have minimal stretch and higher sensitivity to lure movement. They often have a smooth coating and are highly abrasion-resistant. BRUCE CURTIS

As for the terminal section of your line, the leader, you don't need to get into heavier stuff until you fish for sizable game or around rough structure. In light freshwater situations, a 10-inch section of monofilament with slightly greater breaking strength (meaning it will hold a greater load) than the main line is fine. Super-low-visibility fluorocarbon leaders come into play with very careful freshwater fish like trout.

When you fish for big bass, pike, muskie, large catfish, and salmon, consider using a leader section that can stand up against hard strikes, toothy mouths, rough scales, and sharp fins. Several different kinds of pre-rigged leaders can also be bought retail. Heavier monofilament and fluorocarbon—from 15- to 100-pound test or higher—nylon-coated steel, titanium, or wire cable form the strong, abrasion-resistant leaders necessary for big fish.

Sinkers and Floats

Fish can be found almost anywhere in the water column. They can feed inches below the surface, or they can hug the bottom. They might work the edges of fast, deep water or glide along a slow, shallow eddy. Getting bait to the right depth for those fish calls for smart use of sinkers and floats.

For most freshwater fishing, a selection of every kind of sinker you'll need can be bought at any sporting goods store. BRUCE CURTIS

Sinkers come in many different forms. Some are designed to hold bottom, while others allow the line to have some freedom of movement. They come in so many gradations of weight that you can carefully fine-tune the amount necessary to find the right depth without negatively affecting the performance of the line or rig.

More and more sinkers are now made from steel, tungsten, bismuth, or brass instead of lead. These materials are slightly more expensive than lead.

Floats are made from hollow plastic or very light wood and are often referred to as "bobbers." Fishing with a round bobber puts the most resistance on a bait. This can work with fish that are hungry and grabbing the bait hard, but with much more wary fish, a slimmer-profile float is the right choice. Floats can be rigged as fixed floats (no line movement) or slip floats that allow some line movement.

Hooks

Each fishing technique has its specific hook type, and baitfishing is no different. Most hooks are made from high-carbon steel, while others are made from stainless steel or alloys. Single hooks are almost universally used with bait or soft plastics, while treble hooks are found on artificial lures, such as plugs and crankbaits.

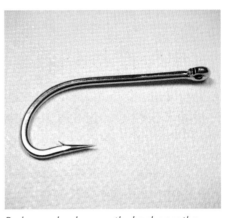

Barbs on a hook secure the hook once the point has penetrated the fish's mouth. Barb size depends on the fish species pursued, with larger, stronger fish calling for more prominent barbs. If you're planning on releasing your fish, it's a good idea to use a hemostat to press the barbs flat. DAVID DIRKS

The hook size of the single hooks used for baitfishing depends on the diameter (or gauge) of the wire used to make it. Fine wire makes small, light hooks for lighter game such as panfish, and works best for dry flies. Medium-gauge wire produces hooks for a variety of game fish, from little bass up to smaller saltwater species. Heavy-gauge wire is used for the biggest species.

Some hooks have an offset bend, left or right, to prevent the hook from spinning when fished with bait in current. And most hook types have a specific name: Sproat (straight point), Aberdeen (round bend, light wire), salmon egg (very short shank), and claw (bait hook with offset point curved inward).

General freshwater hooks range from size 1 to 12, with fly hooks going as high as 24—the higher the number, the smaller the hook.

SWIVELS AND SNAPS

While the best way to connect sections of line or to tie leaders to lures is usually with a good knot, there are times when a quality swivel, snap, or the combination snap-swivel is just the thing. In a typical swivel or snap, each ring end turns on a vertical axis. This is helpful when the action of a lure or baited hook, or the pull of a sinker, would otherwise be putting a twist in the line. The swivel serves as an intermediate connector, often between the leader and main line, and absorbs the torque created by fishing action.

Baits

Earthworms

The worm on a hook is an icon of fishing. Earthworms of various kinds are very good natural baits; the two most popular kinds for fishing are night crawlers and red worms. Night crawlers are preferred for their size—anywhere from 6 to 9 inches—and 3- to 4-inch red worms are often easily found at bait shops. Anglers also use garden worms, a 5- to 6-inch earthworm species found in damp soils, and 3- to 4-inch manure worms, a species found in farmland soils.

To thread a worm onto your hook, pierce it through the collar (the light-colored band behind its head), using a hook with a long shank. It should be as natural-looking and lively as possible on the hook. Don't thread it so far that its body bends with the shank or is otherwise kinked.

Rig an amount of worm appropriate to the fish you're hoping to catch. For smaller fish, a piece of one worm might be enough, while whole night crawlers work well for big bass when fished slowly through cover or along the bottom. Rigging multiple worms is usually a waste insofar as fish will tear into multiple worms, eating much of your bait before they get to the hook point. Don't hook a night crawler in its tail—let that be free to swim and curl, enticing fish.

Nothing says baitfishing quite like earthworms. SHUTTERSTOCK / WAWRITTO

Crayfish

North America is home to dozens of different species of crayfish, ranging from 2 to 6 inches in length. Large-mouth and smallmouth bass readily devour these lobster-like crustaceans, but fishing crayfish can also work well for panfish and, in some situations, trout. Most anglers buy their crayfish at bait shops.

Not unlike catching earthworms, making a game out of finding crayfish can provide another entrée into the sport for the next generation. SHUTTERSTOCK / OLEG DOROSHIN

A crayfish bait must be fished on the bottom to be effective, but a float positioned on the line such that the bait is allowed to reach the bottom can also be used. Fish a crayfish with minimal weight on the line—maybe just one or two very small split shot about 25 inches above the hook. Use a long-shank hook with enough gap for sufficient hook-sets, depending on crayfish size.

Don't hook a crayfish through its main body, as this will injure it and prevent it from staying lively. If casting a crayfish from a boat, affix the hook straight up and down to the tail. If casting from shore, hook the crayfish in the tail lengthwise.

Baitfish

The terms "baitfish" and "forage fish" indicate a species that isn't very high on the food chain. The word "minnow" has become a generic term for any small (1- to 4-inch) freshwater baitfish, but this includes chubs, dace, true minnows, shiners, and sculpins—fish of a wide variety of colors and shapes.

Often, the largest local game fish will primarily eat baitfish or small game fish, including shiners, sunfish, and shad. Smallmouth bass and big trout inhale sculpins and dace, and crappie and walleye attack minnows. Channel catfish and flathead catfish eat any fish

The common dace makes for an effective baitfish. SHUTTERSTOCK / NIKITIN VICTOR

they can get in their mouths. Pike and muskie are much the same, and also eat their own kind. Smaller minnows fished on size 8 or perhaps size 10 hooks work for sunfish, perch, and crappie.

Crappie, walleye, and smallmouth bass anglers probably make the most active and frequent use of minnows as bait, and often carry aerated live-wells on their boats to keep minnows fresh and active.

Hook a live minnow in a way that won't interfere with its ability to swim. Affix the hook in a minnow's tail, dorsal fin, or back, and in shallow waters, fish it on enough line to let it move naturally along the bottom. In deeper water, use a light float to set the minnow to depth. Dead minnows can be rigged for cast-and-retrieve or trolling by using the leader to secure them. Pass the leader through the gill and down the body, or through the gill and wrapped once around the body.

Insect Baits

Being opportunistic feeders, fish won't turn down most insects, and given the incredible variety of bugs that flourish in or around streams and lakes, there are many different kinds of insect baits the angler can use. While some of these baits can be store-bought, often you can collect insects readily in natural settings.

Insects must be rigged as unobtrusively and fished as naturally as possible, with hooks that aren't too large and that allow the bug to be lively. Insects that land on the surface, such as beetles and grasshoppers, should, of course, be fished on the surface, while aquatic insect baits (like large nymphs) should be fished along the bottom. Bugs that can be readily placed on a hook include beetles, wax worms and grubs, grasshoppers, crickets, and hellgrammites, among others.

Crickets, hooked shallow behind the head (point up), can be drifted subsurface with a small split shot. DAVID DIRKS

Grasshoppers attract panfish, trout, and bass. Hook them through the collar and fish them on the surface using a very light leader. If needed, a small bobber can give weight for a cast. Crickets, hooked shallow behind the head, point up, can be drifted subsurface with a small split shot to trout and bass.

Hellgrammites, the nymphs (larvae) of the dobsonfly, are found under stream rocks and are a primo smallmouth bait. Hook a hellgrammite shallowly through its collar, but beware its pincer jaws. Affix enough split shot to the line to get the nymph near the bottom. Use a float to keep it off the bottom.

Fish beetles under tree limbs or near reeds. Larger beetles can be rigged just like hoppers and fished on the surface, using a small bobber.

Canned Food

For years, artificial and homemade baits have been used in lieu of natural ones, mostly targeted at catfish, carp, panfish, and trout. Many of these baits arise from old recipes involving dough and cheese for catfish, and dough, cheese, and corn-kernel baits for trout. Contemporary processed baits are fished in their own way, often with bottom rigs, but the approach is the same as it is for not-real baits: Get the baited hook into the fish's strike zone.

Salmon eggs can be fished singly or in pairs, just above the bottom or drifted in current. DAVID DIRKS

Technically speaking, salmon eggs are a naturally occurring bait, but the salmon eggs you buy in the bait shop have been culled, cured, and are often colored and sometimes flavored, so they are quite a bit removed from their natural state. These processed eggs are used mainly for trout and salmon fishing. Dough balls (cornmeal, flour, and water, sometimes with syrup added) and egg sacks (coming in fishnet bags, presented to look like fresh roe) make for good baits as well.

SCENTS

A lot of debate surrounds the use of scents on fish baits. Some people swear by them, while others scoff. Catfish and carp baits almost universally have some kind of odor, and all natural baits put some scent in the water. Many soft plastics come "scent-impregnated" and really reek. If your own experience suggests that scent makes a difference with the species you pursue, stick with it.

Making Casts

Accuracy

Accuracy comes from the baitcasting angler's ability to manipulate the duration of the cast. And while few people can pick up a baitcaster and make proficient casts right away (the timing and coordination of baitcasting give it

To start your baitcast toss, use your wrist and forearm to take the rod tip from 9 to 11 o'clock, stopping the rod without going over your shoulder. Start your forward stroke with your thumb tight to the light. Your thumb will leave the spool briefly as you finish the forward stroke and the lure takes flight. DAVID DIRKS

Once the rod unloads, put your thumb into contact with the spool to control the lure. When the lure nears its target, press your thumb into the spool until it stops. DAVID DIRKS

a bit of a learning curve), the accuracy that comes from using your thumb to regulate the spool and outflow of line is tough to match with other tackle.

Practice casting with the rod, reel, line, and lures that you intend to fish with the most. If you have a reel that comes with a built-in spool-braking system, which slows the spool's spinning right at the very end of the cast to prevent overrun ("backlash"), turn this system to its lowest setting or disengage it entirely so that you're learning from an unfettered spool.

Spool Control

Place the index finger of your casting hand around the handle or trigger grip, and press your thumb to the spool. The spool-release clutch, if your reel has one, should be right under your thumb.

Rotate the casting hand inward slightly so the knuckle of your index finger points upward. This slight turning of the casting hand allows the wrist to flex and do the necessary work. Using just wrist and forearm, take the rod tip from 9 to 11 o'clock, stopping the rod without going over your shoulder. Be sure the rod fully flexes, or "loads," putting a bend in it at the top of the cast.

Your thumb leaves the spool briefly as you finish the forward stroke and the lure takes flight. Once the rod unloads and the lure is moving, immediately put your thumb into contact with the spool to control the lure. As the lure arcs downward to the target, press your thumb back into the spinning spool to control the lure's drop. When the lure is just about to reach the target, press your thumb into the spool until it stops.

Most anglers switch hands after the cast—the casting hand moves to the crank, and the other hand holds the rod.

After you've made your cast, try switching hands. Move your casting hand to the crank, and the other hand to the rod grip. DAVID DIRKS

Flipping

The sidearm, underhand, and flip casts that work for spinning and spincasting outfits can also be readily accomplished by the baitcasting angler. In fact, along with mastering spool control, these approaches can produce highly accurate lure placement, despite the angler being crowded by brush or having to cast around tree limbs.

Baitcasting reels matched to the right rod also offer another excellent technique: "flipping." This technique, which arose out of largemouth bass fishing, uses a short, pendulum-like cast to deliver a weighted soft-plastic lure or jig to heavy cover, usually from a boat. With this method, an angler can tuck the lure right into a spot where he thinks a bass might be waiting.

Flipping requires two-handed coordination. The casting hand works the rod, and the other hand handles the line. This is a technique that works only with a lure that has enough weight to carry the pendulum action of the cast—a jig or weighted worm.

Flipping does not cover distance—it's an accuracy cast—so get close to the target. Stand to make the cast, and let out as much line as the rod is long, up to 8 feet. Use your free hand to draw line off the reel, holding it between your thumb and index finger, stopping your hand just off your hip. Dip the rod tip as you pull back the outgoing line with your free hand, extending your arm. Raise the rod tip again, building up speed, and swing the lure (think of a wrecking ball) forward to the target. As the lure swings forward, move your free hand forward, letting the line shoot between your index finger and thumb. Finish the cast by pointing the rod at the target, extending it as necessary to reach the target. To pitch the lure to another spot, point the rod at the lure and grab the line with your free hand. Pull the line with your hand as you raise the rod, turn to face the new target, and swing the line like the lure is a wrecking ball.

> ## THE FLIPPIN' SWITCH
> Some baitcasting reels have a "flippin' switch," which allows you to flip with just your casting hand. Engage the flippin' switch and depress the spool clutch; line pays out but the gears are still engaged.

Chapter Three

Spincasting Basics

Fishing with spinning and spincasting outfits is very easy, this being the main reason for their wide popularity. You need minimal ability to learn how to cast, and the skills you acquire come quickly and can be rapidly improved upon. Of course, when you're propelling fish hooks through the air at 40 miles per hour, you do need to take a bit of care to do it right.

Lures

Hard-Body Lures

There are probably more makes and models of artificial lures than there are brands of beer. The creation of various twentieth-century plastics brought about light-bodied, high-performance lures that look and act a lot like baitfish, worms, amphibians, and crustaceans.

Numerous lures are species-specific, while others attract strikes from any kind of fish. Spinnerbaits are mostly intended for various bass species and secondarily for pickerel and pike. You won't see many catfish caught on a spinnerbait, but a single spoon in the right color can nab trout, bass, pike, and salmon.

A good tackle box is packed and prepped for any eventuality. SHUTTERSTOCK / ARENA CREATIVE; FACING PAGE: SHUTTERSTOCK / ALEXEY LOSEVICH

Crankbaits

Used to target bass found at specific depths, crankbaits imitate a fleeing baitfish. Such lures are made of plastic or balsa wood and can incorporate internal, rattling noisemakers. The size of the lip of the crankbait determines its diving depth: The larger the lip, the deeper the dive.

Most crankbaits are designed to wobble while "cranked." DAVID DIRKS

Lipless Crankbaits

Often used to search for feeding fish, lipless crankbaits can be fished with varying speeds and retrieves. These lures are usually fitted with very loud internal rattles to send out vibrations similar to those of moving baitfish. The body design of lipless crankbaits gives them a fast wobble.

Lipless crankbaits come in a variety of colors and patterns. DAVID DIRKS

Poppers

Meant to be fished on the surface, the concave face of a popper throws up a small splash of water and makes a distinctive popping sound—action that is meant to imitate a terrestrial (like a small frog) or a wounded baitfish.

Surface lures, like poppers, are highly effective for largemouth bass after sundown. DAVID DIRKS

Plugs

Longer hard-bodied lures that float or sink slowly and are reeled in with a steady retrieve are often referred to generically as "plugs" or "minnow-style" baits. Floating models dive and dip off the surface, while sinking models drop to a desired depth and are then cranked through the strike zone.

This plug has a solid body, but some of them have jointed bodies that waggle attractively during a retrieve. DAVID DIRKS

Spinners, Spoons, and Jigs

Spinners, spoons, and jigs are some of the oldest lure designs in America. Spoons are probably the most simple of all—just an oblong, rounded piece of light, thin metal. They have a lively wobble when fished and mostly imitate a fleeing baitfish.

Spinners also imitate baitfish, with a metallic or plastic blade that spins rapidly around the wire shaft of the lure.

Jigs come in a tremendous variety but have a basic configuration: a metal head (usually lead) fused to a hook, with an attached body of bucktail, feather, or soft plastic.

If you are retrieving your spinner too slowly, or if it's fouled with debris or tangled in some way, you may feel it in the line itself. A properly retrieved spinner often communicates a nice thrum up the line. DAVID DIRKS

Spinners

Spinners incorporate silver-, copper-, or chrome-plated blades and stainless steel main shafts. Most spinners have one treble hook and can be dressed with feathers or fur to create a flowing skirt around the hooks. Spinners have to be retrieved fast enough to get the blade spinning.

Spoons

Spoons made for casting and retrieving can also often be trolled, and some spoons are meant to be "jigged" (retrieved

Many spoon patterns have imitation eyes either painted on them or, in the case of beads, affixed. DAVID DIRKS

vertically). Spoons can have a finish as simple as stamped, silver-plated brass or have inlaid holographic reflectors. Most spoons are fitted with a single treble hook, but some come with a single hook with a weed guard.

Jigs

Small jigs—from ¹⁄₃₂ to ¹⁄₁₆ ounce— in all kinds of colors, and sometimes fit with spinning blades, target panfish, perch, and trout. Bucktail jigs from ¹⁄₄₄ to ³⁄₈ ounce

Jigs are especially effective when slow, probing fishing is necessary—something that quick-swimming lures can't handle. DAVID DIRKS

work well for larger perch, smallmouth bass, and walleye. Jig heads vary greatly in shape, from round to football or bullet shaped.

Largemouth Bass-Specific Jigs

Largemouth bass-specific jigs feature big, blossoming latex skirts and heavy weed guards. These jigs are intended for casts to thick cover, such as weeds and lily pads, and swim toward the bottom with a lot of motion. The swirling, pulsating skirt on such a jig is what entices strikes from largemouth bass. Fish such a jig

Like most freshwater lures, bass-specific jigs come in a variety of styles and colors. DAVID DIRKS

in a yo-yo fashion, getting it to rise and then drop to maximize the action of the skirt.

ICE FISHING

Jigs and spoons play a major role in ice fishing, in which they are fished vertically by raising and dropping the rod tip, with minimal use of the reel. Ice-fishing-specific spoons and jigs are often Day-Glo colored with highly iridescent finishes.

Spinnerbaits, Buzzbaits, and Plastics

Anyone who has watched professional bass fishing knows how big a role spinnerbaits, buzzbaits, and soft-plastic baits play in that endeavor. Just about every serious bass angler has a wide assortment of these highly versatile lures.

Spinnerbaits and buzzbaits don't look like any kind of natural bait. Their flash, motion, and sound are what induce strikes. Spinnerbaits can be fished shallow or deep, fished to the bottom and jigged up, or fished in a stop-and-go fashion. They can nab smallmouth bass, crappie, pickerel, and pike, as well as largemouth bass. Buzzbaits ride in the surface tension and their propellers spin, making noise and commotion. These lures are mainly for targeting largemouth.

Soft-plastic lures can be either near-replicas of various natural foods (worms, frogs, and fish) or alien-like things with tentacles that swirl and squiggle in the water. There's a soft-plastic lure for every situation and most major game fish. Such lures work very well in heavy cover, but you can also jig them, crawl or bounce them along the bottom, or do a yo-yo retrieve (up and down).

> ## SPINNERBAITS
>
> - Color choice is a major consideration, but finding the right depth to fish a spinnerbait is just as important.
>
> - Most spinnerbaits use willow leaf or Colorado blades, singly or in combinations, and blade size and color have a significant impact on fish attraction.
>
> - Anglers often affix a soft-plastic grub or worm section to a spinnerbait hook, in the center of the skirt.
>
> - Spinnerbaits should swim without wobble and can be "tuned" by bending the body wire to achieve this.

Buzzbaits

Use buzzbaits to search out bass in muddy waters or when other lures don't produce. Pick a buzzbait that can be fished as slow as possible but with the blades still turning and spitting water. Use darker colors for murky water and light colors in sun.

Bass that short-strike a buzzbait can be nabbed by adding a single trailer hook to the main hook. DAVID DIRKS

Plastic Worms

Bass can be caught on plastic worms of various sizes, but in general the longer worms take the bigger fish. Plastic worms come in a huge variety of colors—picking the right color requires a little research and trial and error. A worm's body shape, tail configuration, and thickness often determine how you'll fish it.

Suppleness in a worm is important. Older worms can sometimes become stiff and brittle. Don't be afraid to replace them if they're showing some wear and tear. DAVID DIRKS

Various Soft Plastics

Flipping a big, ugly soft plastic into heavy cover has become a major tactic of largemouth bass fishing. Dragging a tube bait over the bottom or over rocks and structure is a highly effective approach for smallmouth. Soft-plastic "jerkbaits" look like worms with a fattened belly but are designed to dart and drop, imitating a wounded baitfish.

Many soft plastics are scent-impregnated with natural ingredients so they really stink. DAVID DIRKS

Plastic Worm Rigs

The plastic worm has long been a mainstay of bass fishing. Rigging a worm in various ways can capitalize on its suppleness and swimming characteristics. Worms work best in warm water and warm weather, and for casting to specific bass lairs or to fish at a particular depth.

When fishing these rigs, work them slowly to give the worm a chance to slither and dance. When bass take a plastic worm, the sensation is more like a quick thud or rap on your line; the fish inhale the slow-moving worm, as opposed to striking hard.

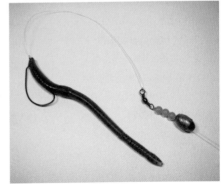

A Carolina rig should be slowly retrieved along the bottom. DAVID DIRKS

Carolina Rig

Hook a worm through its head with a worm hook and embed the point.

Tie 20 inches of leader from the hook eye to a barrel swivel. Push the main line through a cone-head or barrel sinker, then through a bead or two, and then tie the end of the main line to the top eye of the swivel.

Texas Rig
Hook a worm through its head with a worm hook, embedding the point. Tie a leader to the hook eye; the worm can simply be fished this way weightless, if desired. For weight, slide a cone-head sinker down the leader to the hook eye.

Work a Texas rig through shallow cover. DAVID DIRKS

Wacky-Worm Rig
The wacky-worm rig often involves a thick, shorter worm with evenly tapered ends. Hook the worm through the center of its body, or cinch a small rubber O-ring around the worm and slip the hook through that. Use a light 20-inch leader tied to a small barrel swivel and as light a main line as possible.

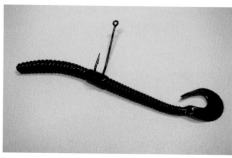

Let the wacky worm slowly descend without any rod motion, then give it light twitches with a slow retrieve. DAVID DIRKS

Drop-Shot Worm
Tie on one or two hooks with dropper or Palomar knots directly to the main line. Tie the end of the main line directly to a casting or bell sinker heavy enough to hold bottom. Pick a worm that flutters in the water, and hook it through the nose.

When fishing a drop-shot worm, drop the sinker to the bottom, keeping an almost vertical connection while lightly vibrating the line with the rod tip (don't lift the sinker). COURTESY OF LURENET.COM

Making Casts

Rod Action

One of the most common mistakes in casting with a spinning reel is not flipping the bail completely open. When this happens, the line remains secured and you will most likely snap off your lure. The same will happen in spincasting if you fail to depress the line-release button completely and then try to cast.

With a spinning reel, you can keep your index finger extended to brush it against the spool and slow or stop a bad cast. With a spincaster, you can place your free hand alongside the reel as you cast and tender the line with your index finger.

Flexible rods require a slightly slower casting action than stiffer rods, but you might be able to cast more accurately with a stiffer rod. Before purchasing a rod, test-cast a number of them (with the reel you intend to use on the rod) to see what kind of length and flex you prefer.

Use the index finger of your grip hand to secure the line for casting. Next, use your other hand to flip open the bail. With 4 or 5 inches of line hanging from the tip of the rod, move your rod tip from 9 to 11 o'clock, stopping the rod motion and letting the line slip off your finger. When the lure is in the water, flip the bail back to prepare it for a retrieve. DAVID DIRKS

Casting Action

To cast with a spinning reel, use the index finger of your grip hand to secure the line for casting. Use your other hand to flip open the bail. Grab the line with your index finger before you flip the bail, or the weight of the lure will pull out line.

Have roughly 4 or 5 inches of line hanging from the tip of the rod in preparation to cast. Casting will be a quick hammering motion from about 9 to 11 o'clock high and back. Start the cast by looking at your target, and keep your eye on it as you complete the cast. Stop the forward motion when the rod tip points slightly higher than the target, and let the line slip off your finger.

If using a spincasting outfit, keep the line-release button depressed under your thumb through the entire cast. Start the cast with 4 or 5 inches of line hanging from the tip of the rod. Keep your index finger secure in the trigger grip (on the underside of the rod) throughout the cast; this helps with controlling rod motion. The cast motion is a hammering-a-nail stroke, moving the rod from roughly 9 o'clock to 11 o'clock and back. Release the push button just as you complete the cast and are aiming the rod tip slightly above the target.

Mastering Casts

The "9 to 11 o'clock" casting arc assumes that you have enough open space around you to work the rod over the shoulder of your casting arm. Such optimal situations, however, are not always possible. Once you're on the water, you'll have to deal with tree limbs, brush, and distance. As you get more comfortable with your various rods and reels, and start to hone your skills, you will be able to adapt your casting methods.

Two-handed Spincasting

Two-handed spincasting can give better control and impart greater accuracy and power. Fit the palm of your least dominant hand along the reel body or at the base of the handle—whichever gives you better control. Use your index finger to feather the line after your thumb lets up the line-release button. The motion for both arms is still basically the same: all wrist, forearm, and elbow action—no shoulder or raising the upper arms.

Sidearm Cast

Use this cast around brush and limbs or when the wind is strong enough to hinder an overhead cast. Arc the sidearm the same as in the overhead cast, about 9 to 11 o'clock, but position it flat and out to the casting-arm side. Don't open up your arm from the elbow much—flex your wrist as you turn your hand outward to make the cast.

If you're having trouble casting with only one hand, try the two-handed approach.
DAVID DIRKS

A sidearm cast can help clear brush and limbs. DAVID DIRKS

Underhand Cast

If you're on a riverbank, with space below you but limited space above and to the side, hold the rod in front of you, angled down, and then flex it upward with wrist action to about 10 o'clock. Keep the line-release button depressed, or the line around your index fingers, as you stroke the rod downward so the tip points at the water. Bring the rod upward briskly, and as the rod comes almost level, release the button or the line from your finger (with a spinning reel).

Flip Cast

Use this approach in thick cover. Start out as if making a brisk sidearm cast and quickly build up speed, but then stop halfway through. Rotate your wrist down and back around (forward) in a quick snap so the rod tip travels in a fast, tight semicircle. As your wrist comes back around, point the rod at the target and release the line.

SUNGLASSES

Regardless of how bright the sun is, always wear sunglasses or eye protection when fishing. Casts can go awry or snagged lures can suddenly come flying back at you, and a hook in the eye makes for a bad day.

When buying your sunglasses, make sure the lenses are polarized. The polarization helps cut down on glare and reflection from the water surface, giving you a better chance of seeing the fish before they see you.

Sunglasses are not only a safety consideration: Their polarization can also be a factor in determining your day's success. SHUTTERSTOCK / ELZBIETA SEKOWSKA

Chapter Four

Fly-Fishing Basics

Among the various style of freshwater fishing discussed, fly fishing has the steepest learning curve. For the beginning angler, it can be a daunting prospect, picking up a fly rod, making the first attempts at a cast. On the surface, it should be a simple thing, to send a heavier line and a lighter tippet in a rolling arc to drop a fly flat on the water. But not unlike a golf swing, or perhaps hitting a good backhand tennis shot, the actuality is much different than the appearance.

But once you have a grasp on the basics of fly fishing, the potential to challenge yourself, to become progressively more skillful, is almost infinite. From matching the hatch with a tiny mayfly to dead-drifting a nymph down a riffle or dredging streamers from a boat, you can fly fish your entire life and still find ways to improve. For those who like to challenge themselves, to change and grow into a sport, this is the style of fishing to pursue.

SHUTTERSTOCK / DEC HOGAN

Flies

Although the lure on the end of a fly line can range from a tiny puff of feather to a length of surgical tubing shaped into a baitfish, both of these lures and everything between these limits of design can be called a "fly." Flies are measured on a scale that matches standard, even-numbered hook sizes, from 2 (big) to 28 (very small) for freshwater flies, and 0 (pretty big) to 4/0 (bigger) for saltwater flies.

The great advantage to flies is that if an angler also knows how to tie a fly (an art all its own), he or she can perfectly match the lure to the actual natural creature. And unlike buying lures in a store, if you can tie flies, you can make the thing exactly as you think it should be made.

Discussions of flies tied to imitate various insects often refer to "artificials" (the lure) and "naturals" (the actual, real bug). A "recipe" is a formal set of ingredients for tying a particular fly, resulting in a "pattern" of definitive color and configuration usually identified by a proper name; for example, Black Ghost streamer, Griffith's Black Gnat, or Olive Woolly Bugger. Materials used to tie flies range from feathers of special chicken breeds to squirrel fur to Styrofoam. Saltwater fly patterns often incorporate small metal heads (like jigs) to sink the fly faster and farther.

A good fly box will have several duplicates of the essential, general flies, as well as a rotating series of specific flies that anticipate the day ahead. SHUTTERSTOCK / PATRICIA HOFMEESTER

Dry Flies

Dry flies imitate various winged aquatic insects (newly hatched or adults) sitting on the water's surface. Most dry flies range from a size 12 to a size 22, but can get even smaller to imitate the tiniest aquatic insects. Dry flies must be fished "drag free," requiring careful slack management and line mending. "Matching the hatch"—a popular catchphrase—involves comparing a dry fly to a natural to see if it is a close imitation.

When fishing a dry fly, always coat it first with a commercially available floatant. A dab of silicone gel will keep the fly riding high in the water. DAVID DIRKS

Nymph Patterns

Nymph patterns imitate the larval, or nymphal, stage of aquatic insects and are fished in the water column or along the bottom. Nymphs are sometimes tied with a metal bead-head (which possibly resembles an air bubble) that can help sink the fly in current. When there's no insect hatch occurring, nymph patterns can be used to locate trout.

Fish feed more consistently on nymphs than dry flies. When you don't see fish rising, consider going to a nymph. DAVID DIRKS

Bass Bugs

When retrieved with a stop-and-go action, bass bugs can mimic a baitfish fleeing on the surface or a swimming frog. Some bass bugs have cupped faces to make a popping sound, while others have bullet-shaped bodies for subtler noisemaking. Being heavier than most flies, some bass bugs benefit from fly lines designed specifically for them.

Bass like their flies big, colorful, and ugly. DAVID DIRKS

Smaller bass-bug-style patterns in black, white, and bumblebee colors work very well for big sunfish.

Streamers

Streamers can be tied with a variety of materials and are mainly intended to imitate various baitfish species. The word "streamer" refers to a freshwater fly, but many saltwater patterns are simply beefed-up, streamer-like flies. Most streamers are fished from mid-depths to the bottom and retrieved with quick strips of the line. Just about any streamer can be weighted so it sinks faster, especially in fast currents, and rides just over the bottom.

Streamers can be either fished on the retrieve (jerking them back in 6-inch "strips") or, in current, dead-drifted along. DAVID DIRKS

BASIC FLIES

While advanced fly fishers will usually have boxes full of flies meant specifically to match a certain hatch, the bulk of the angler's time will be spent fishing flies that more generally imitate a class of bugs rather than a specific insect. When nymphing for trout, always carry a Prince Nymph or a Bead-Head Prince. For dry flies, a Royal Wulff is meant to imitate any number of insects. And you should always carry a bunch of Woolly Buggers with you in olive, brown, and black. These flies are technically streamers, and no one knows exactly what fish mistake them for—maybe big nymphs, leeches, or crayfish—but they are highly effective patterns for both trout and bass. Fish a Woolly Bugger either on a dead-drift or retrieved like a streamer.

Making Casts

Basic Rod Work

The first few times you try fly casting, you'll probably have line lashed everywhere, but the basic motion will start coming to you sooner than you think. Imagine a wooden dowel with a long piece of very light string attached to the end; flick that dowel back and forth, between 10 and 1 o'clock, using just your arm and elbow, and watch how the string forms the same shape—a flat line with a tight loop at the end—going backward and then forward. That's the basis of every cast, and it starts with the backcast.

A basic fly cast needs a lot more room than a cast with a spinning outfit. The line unfurls straight out behind you prior to the angler starting his forward cast. DAVID DIRKS

To learn the motion, extend about 20 feet of line from the end of the rod, take up the proper grip and stance, and simply work the rod back and forth, keeping the line in the air. Don't try to force it or go quickly, and be sure to stop the rod at a near-vertical position. The more line you have in the air, the more time you must give to the backcast—the backward motion of the rod that pulls all the line from in front of you and transfers it behind you, and thus loads the rod for the forward cast.

Proper Rod Grip

Hold the rod handle with your thumb on top; keep your wrist in line with your forearm. The tip-top of the rod should be at eye level, with line out in front of you, as you make the backcast. Keep your elbow slightly away from your body, about 2 or 3 inches, and your biceps almost touching. Raise the rod swiftly

A good fly cast starts with a good grip. DAVID DIRKS

and smoothly, your thumb knuckle coming up almost in line with your ear and your wrist straight (as if hammering).

The Backcast
The elbow is the pivot point of making the backcast and forward cast. Don't tilt your wrist backward at the end of the backcast; keep it in line with your forearm as you stop the rod at 12 o'clock. You must wait for the backcast to unroll behind you before you come forward; this pause gets longer with more line. When you feel the line load the rod with a slight tug, that's when your arm should come forward.

The Forward Cast
The "hammer and nail" motion will be most clear on the forward cast; keep your wrist and forearm straight. Speed up the rod as you come from 12 o'clock down to eye level again, using your forearm and shoulder to power the stroke. If your elbow comes away from your body a little bit, that's all right. Finish the cast crisply with a bit of hand strength, but keep your wrist locked—don't cock it downward.

Most fly casts need a stiff wrist throughout. Let your elbow do the work. DAVID DIRKS

A good cast will have a rolling "loop" in the line that unrolls toward your casting target.
DAVID DIRKS

Completing the Cast

As you finish the cast, use your hand to aim the tip-top just slightly above the target. Cast the line out over the water, not into the water, so that it falls evenly as the loop of leader unrolls. If your forward cast comes forward sloppily, the line probably touched the ground behind you because you opened your wrist on the backcast. If the cast collapses completely, you didn't pause long enough for the backcast.

If you're fishing dry flies on the surface, it's usually important to land them on the water with as soft a presentation as possible. Wet flies can be sloppier. DAVID DIRKS

Advanced Casting

Manipulating a fly line as you make a cast and while it's on the water are often necessities, frequently having to do with the varying speeds and directions of current, and streamside cover. Other times, you'll manipulate the fly line to increase line speed and thus improve your distance.

Discussed here are four major line-control techniques for freshwater: the roll cast, for when there's too much cover behind you for a normal backcast; line mending, to reduce current drag on the leader and fly; the slack cast, to throw slack into the line before it lands on moving water; and the double haul, a way to impart more speed and distance to your line. Each method has its nuances, but the fundamentals are easy to comprehend. The double haul will seem tricky, but basically you shorten the line with your line hand on the backcast by "hauling," or pulling on it; you then put line into the backcast and then haul the line (shortening it) again on the forward cast.

The Roll Cast

When you don't have room for a backcast, put the rod tip as far behind you as you can (lower than normal), with the line on the water alongside you and extending outward. Your rod hand should be a bit below your shoulder. Stop the rod behind you so the line stops on the water. You need the surface tension to load the rod. Make a normal forward cast, which will unroll the line off the water.

Mending Line on a Stream

Whether fishing dry flies on the surface or wet flies underneath, it's important to keep a tight line. When you see a strike—either a fish hitting your fly on the surface, or your line or indicator bobbing down—you need to be able to quickly set the hook. And setting the hook is difficult, if not impossible, if there is too much slack in the line.

When fishing in moving water, make an upstream mend with a quick, smooth roll of the rod (like a slow jump rope) that picks up the bowed section of line and drops it up-current. You should try to leave just a bit of slack in the leader, resulting in a drag-free fly. When any fly (dry or wet) starts dragging as it drifts, it looks unnatural and will thus be less effective. Streamers, which are meant to be actively retrieved, are the obvious exception to this rule.

A mend is essential for taking the unnecessary slack out of your line. DAVID DIRKS

Throwing a Slack Cast

In certain situations—perhaps you're fishing upstream of a rising fish, and you need to anticipate the drift—you will need to make a cast that intentionally has slack line. To begin, strip a length of line off the reel, pinch the line with your index finger against the rod handle, and make a cast. As the line flows forward, release the slack line and wiggle the tip of the rod sideways before you finish the forward cast. Complete the cast by bringing the rod tip down parallel to the water, as this will maintain the slack in the line. The line should fall evenly on the water in a slack-filled squiggle shape.

MAKE IT EASY

Similar to a driving range, you can set up a fly-casting practice course using plastic rings of about 14 inches in diameter. Place these on the ground at different distances, and work at different casting techniques while trying to land a practice fly (point and barb removed) in the ring. Hang a ring from a tree limb about 5 feet above the ground and practice putting the fly through it.

The Double Haul

To throw more line than with a typical cast, start a backcast with no slack in the line and the line in your line hand. As you raise the rod, haul the line down past your waist with your line hand (shortening the entire line). As the rod reaches vertical, with the line flowing behind you, bring your line hand up almost level to your rod hand. On the forward stroke, haul the line down past your waist again, and then release it as you finish the forward stroke.

The double haul—while admirable as a casting accomplishment—is rarely necessary in freshwater fishing. Learn it, then save it for your bonefishing trip to the Bahamas. DAVID DIRKS

A brown trout and a big pike in a mountain lake. SHUTTERSTOCK / KLETR

Chapter Five

Fish Types and Fishing Methods

Each species of freshwater fish will respond to certain fishing methods and approaches. To find the greatest success, the smart angler customizes his tackle and techniques to suit both the fish and the habitat.

Every species of fish has its own predictable habits and habitats. The smart angler tailors his or her methods to the species at hand. Northern pike aren't known as jumpers, but the one in this photo is doing his best. SHUTTERSTOCK / REGINA PRYANICHNIKOVA

Largemouth and Smallmouth Bass

Bass! For experienced fishermen, even the word conjures up exciting images. Balletic leaps! Lunkers sulking down deep! Hard takes and pulled hooks and the satisfaction of the day's best fish held up for a camera. More people pursue largemouth bass in America than any other fish, and the smallmouth bass has long been heralded as one of the most terrific fighters in freshwater.

Between these two species, bass fishing is available almost everywhere in the continental US. Largemouth are found from New England to California, although they do not thrive above the 42nd parallel. And while they prefer

Largemouth bass tend to have bulkier heads and a more rotund gut than smallmouth bass. SHUTTERSTOCK / STEVENRUSSELLSMITHPHOTOS

Once hooked, smallmouth bass are known to be great fighters.
SHUTTERSTOCK / STEVE OEHLENSCHLAGER

warmer, still waters—lakes, ponds, and reservoirs—they also inhabit the slowest waters of warm rivers. Smallmouth thrive best in cool (even cold) rivers and streams and big northern lakes. They are often found near trout water, but not in many places in the South or Southwest. Smallmouth that inhabit larger, nutrient-filled waters can reach some size—a 6-pound smallmouth is a big one.

The Differences

Body markings vary, but most largemouth have a stripe of black splotches down their lateral line and black patches on their cheeks. The corner of a largemouth's jaw extends past the back of its eye socket, a key identifying feature. In terms of habitat, largemouth prefer thick cover in lakes or ponds, an essential part of their ambush method of predation. They can tolerate temperatures from about 35 degrees Fahrenheit up to 90 degrees, but prefer 65 to 85 degrees. Spawning can begin in late winter in places where the water warms to 60 degrees, but usually occurs in mid to late spring. Forage fish and smaller game fish comprise most of the largemouth's diet.

Smallmouth have more of a gold-bronze coloration, and vertical olive or brown bars mottling their sides. Some lake-dwelling smallmouth can become quite dark, with a rich, brown tiger-striping. The corner of a smallmouth's jaw does not extend past the back edge of its eye socket. In small and large streams and in deep lakes, smallmouth prefer a rocky or gravel bottom, and in rivers tend to seek slower sections of water along main current seams. In lakes, smallmouth seek the cooler levels and won't be found in warmer surface layers in summer.

Smallmouth and largemouth bass can occur in the same lakes, but they'll seek different habitat. Smallmouth prefer cooler depths, whereas largemouth will be found in warmer, shallower water. Smallmouth also spawn later than largemouth, usually in late spring or in the early summer.

Catching Largemouth

Largemouth bass are very aggressive and will strike at many different kinds of lures and baits. Once hooked, they tend to run quickly for cover. Baitcasting, spinning, and spincasting outfits all work very well for largemouth bass, and a light- to medium-action rod can handle most any situation. Aside from the "flippin' switch" that some baitcaster reels have, any quality reel designed for medium-weight freshwater fishing should be enough to match a largemouth.

Bass are not terribly line shy, but in clear water they can be wary of a heavier line. A 4- to 8-pound monofilament or braided main line will be fine in farm-pond situations. Waters known for larger bass call for an 8- to 12-pound-test line.

A largemouth bass comes out of the water. SHUTTERSTOCK / DCWCREATIONS

Lures

Soft plastics and spinnerbaits can both be used as good fish-searching lures around piers, docks, and other man-made structure. If bass are striking at, but missing, surface plugs, cast a weightless tube bait instead, with a slow, jerky retrieve.

Crankbait can be fished in brush or timber, but slow down your retrieve and stop when the lure bumps a snag, and let it float up. Prospect with spinnerbaits and crankbaits around brush and flooded timber first before casting into the cover.

Natural baits, of course, also work very well for largemouth.

RELEASING BASS

Don't hoist a bass by its lower jaw without also providing support for its body—this can injure important muscles. If you must remove a bass from the water, take hold of its lower jaw simply to secure the fish, but either hold the fish vertically or cradle the bass horizontally with your other hand, putting no weight on the jaw. And always make sure your hands are wet before handling the fish. The slime on a fish (a glycoprotein called mucin) helps protect them in a variety of ways. If you damage the slime with dry hands, it can shorten the fish's life.

Catching Smallmouth

The smallmouth's main diet consists of baitfish, but they also readily eat crayfish and a variety of nymphs, leeches and worms, and various insects. They'll feed through the entire water column, taking insects off the surface and picking crayfish and nymphs off the bottom. Smallmouth will thus respond to a wide variety of lures. Jigs, crankbaits, spinnerbaits, and soft plastics can be highly successful, and so can diving plugs, spoons, and spinners. Natural baits (minnows, crayfish, hellgrammites, and worms) should be fished live, if possible.

Smallmouth are aggressive feeders and will often readily hit spoons, spinners, jigs, flies, and, of course, a variety of baits.

SHUTTERSTOCK / STEVE OEHLENSCHLAGER

Use jigs and crankbaits to locate smallmouth bass in lakes. Successful searches along rocky edges or drop-offs and vertical presentations to deep points often make use of bucktail or plastic-skirted jigs and jig heads fixed with curly-tailed soft plastics. Crankbaits matched to local forage-fish colors or crayfish crank patterns can work well; crayfish-imitating crankbaits need to reach the bottom and flutter along the rocks. In clear waters, bright, rattling crankbaits fished stop-and-go at lower depths are a good searching lure. Crankbait patterns also imitate local forage fish, usually shad and perch, in silver, white, and yellow. A soft-plastic jerkbait retrieved on the surface with quick twitches of the rod can induce very hard smallmouth strikes. Try topwater lures on a very calm lake surface early in the morning and at sundown, varying the speed of the retrieve.

Light spinning and baitcasting outfits work fine for smallmouth, with monofilament or braided line on a lightweight reel. A braided line allows a better touch with jigs fished deep or crankbaits close to the bottom, and a low-visibility fluorocarbon leader in very clear water is a smart move.

Bass Fly Fishing

Long before there were baitcasting outfits and bass boats, people were casting flies to bass. The flies are most often meant to mimic bass's favorite food—baitfish—but can also imitate frogs, leeches, crayfish, and nymphs. A 6- to 8-inch length of brown or red chenille will flutter in the water as nicely as a soft-plastic worm. Poppers are a highly popular fly for both largemouth and small-mouth bass.

Largemouth will readily take frog-patterned and baitfish-patterned poppers cast to lily pads and weed patches. Let a popper sit

When fished correctly, bass poppers make a distinct "popping" noise on the retrieve. DAVID DIRKS

for a short time after it lands on the surface, and then give it a few light pops before slowly stripping it in. Strip a popper in a stop-and-go fashion, pulling the line crisply enough to get the "pop" sound and splash.

Below the surface, big Woolly Buggers in olive, black, or brown will catch a smallmouth's eye, while the same flies ticked along the bottom will also nab largemouth bass. The Clouser Minnow, developed specifically for smallmouth, sinks quickly and swims along the bottom.

Most fly-fishing tackle for largemouth and smallmouth bass is either slow or medium action, with rods and lines from 4- to 8-weight. Fly reels for freshwater bass fishing rarely need much backing, as these fish are brawlers, not long runners.

Panfish

Sunfish

Various sunfish species, such as bluegill and pumpkinseed, are found almost nationwide, inhabiting the shorelines and shallows of ponds, creeks, lakes, and slower rivers, within easy reach of short casts. Given sunfish's preference for shallows, anglers can often sight-cast to them and watch the strike, an added plus for young anglers, who get a good lesson in fish behavior and reaction time. The lightest tackle is all that you need to pursue sunfish.

Within the sunfish family, bluegills usually have greenish bodies with dark vertical bars, an orange breast, and a black-tipped gill cover. A good-size bluegill will reach 10 or 12 inches in length. Pumpkinseeds have turquoise-blue streaks on their heads and many amber and blue spots on the sides. Most pumpkinseeds range from 4 to 8 inches. Redbreast sunfish have a black or blue-black gill point (or "lobe") and are more tapered toward the tail than most sunfish. Redear sunfish possess small teeth and olive-green bodies with numerous dark spots. Redears are found all across the South and into the Midwest and southwest to Texas. They can reach 9 inches or larger in optimal habitat.

Few fish are as easy or as enjoyable for new anglers to catch as bluegill and other panfish.
SHUTTERSTOCK / STEVENRUSSELLSMITHPHOTOS

A wide variety of baits and lures work for sunfish, just as long as they're small enough for the fish to get in their mouths. Hooks much larger than size 6 don't work, with sizes 8 and 10 usually the right choice.

Fishing for Sunfish

A universal sunfish bait rig consists of a small float about 20 inches above a size 8 hook, with two small split shot just below the float. Be careful with hooks much smaller than size 10, as they could be swallowed. Also be aware that sunfish will sometimes peck at a bait before biting it entirely, making the float twitch. Just use a section of a night crawler, as sunfish will pick apart a whole worm before getting to the hook. Wait until the float or bobber moves off steadily or goes under, then set the hook with an easy turn of the wrist.

Standard sunfish jigs have small lead heads and slim nylon or feather skirts; fish these with a medium-fast up-and-down retrieve. Good-size bluegills and redears will chase small grub-tailed jigs and small spinners.

Crappie and Perch

Four major panfish species—black and white crappie, and white and yellow perch—are all premier, light-tackle game fish. The crappie looks a lot like a speckled hybrid of a bass and sunfish, while the white perch (not a true perch) is actually related to the white bass and striped bass. Yellow perch may have some bass-like attributes, but it actually *is* a true perch, in the same family as walleye and sauger.

Black crappies have a gold or olive body covered with irregular bluish or black specks and can sometimes have solid-black backs. The spotted dorsal

Crappie are enthusiastic fighters and not too discerning when it comes to hitting a lure.
SHUTTERSTOCK / DAN THORNBERG

and anal fins are very similar in size and configuration, with seven to eight dorsal spines. They range from 8 to 14 inches and up to 2 pounds. White crappies are lighter colored on their sides than black crappies and have vertical bands of spots covering their silvery-green flanks. With a more tapered and slimmer body than the black crappie, the white crappie can reach 13 or 15 inches.

Yellow perch have an unmistakable yellow-gold body and, during the spawn, bright yellow-orange pelvic and anal fins. Seven or eight vertical brown-black bars extend along the perch's body, from its back almost to its belly. Most yellow perch run 8 to 10 inches and sometimes reach almost 1 pound. They are found in a variety of waters but prefer large, clear lakes, which often makes them a major quarry of ice fishermen. White perch have two dorsal fins and silver-olive or brownish gray backs, with silvery sides and a white belly. Most white perch don't get much larger than 8 or 9 inches. They don't mind brackish water and are often found in estuaries and coastal rivers, but also inhabit inland lakes.

> ## CRAPPIE PRONUNCIATION
>
> The word "crappie" comes from the French-Canadian word *crapet,* used to refer generically to a number of species in the sunfish family, *Centrarchidae,* which includes the black bass. The French *crapet* became "crappe" in early American usage, but its French-Canadian origins are unclear. In some parts of the country, these fish are still referred to with the proper pronunciation—"croppie."

Yellow perch have filled more than one ice fisherman's bucket. SHUTTERSTOCK / KEITH PUBLICOVER

Fishing for Crappie and Perch

Crappie and perch tend to form sizable schools. For crappie, look for deep weeds, brush piles, and drop-offs to deeper water. In hotter weather, black crappies will go deep. White crappies seek the same kinds of structure as black crappies, but not as deep, and don't mind warmer water.

Standard sunfish jigs have small lead heads and slim nylon or feather skirts. Fish them with a medium-fast, up-and-down retrieve. DAVID DIRKS

White perch in brackish waters are often found near the bottom and become active around structure at tide changes. In freshwater lakes, target creek mouths, shelves, or channels between points of land. Sometimes white perch will chase baitfish to the surface. Yellow perch roam open lake water in schools during the day, over a variety of bottoms (rocky, muddy, sand), and need to be prospected for.

The go-to natural bait for crappies is a live minnow hooked through the lip or dorsal fin, fished under a float. Both black and white crappies have tender mouths and don't strike hard. Sometimes slowly trolled rigged minnows (live or dead) can help locate a crappie school.

In terms of artificials, small jigs with curly-tailed soft-plastic grubs work well, while in-line spinners in size 6 or 8 tipped with a soft-plastic minnow is a passable, if larger, lure for crappies. Work jigs, spinners, and spinnerbaits as slowly as possible to get proper swimming action with the lure, but no faster.

Fish lures for yellow perch slowly, getting them near the bottom and keeping them there through the retrieve. Small spinners, small jigs with nylon or hair skirts or tipped with curly-tailed grubs, and very small plugs work well. Cast whole small worms, whole grubs, or live minnows under floats but with enough split shot to get the bait down. Yellow perch holding in very deep water are best approached with a boat so that jigs can be worked vertically.

Searching for white perch often requires a boat in order to cover enough water. In lakes, try small diving plugs. Get lures near the bottom and work them slowly. For baits, drift live minnows and whole small worms under a float with enough line to reach near bottom.

Panfish on the Fly

Fly fishing for panfish can be terrifically fun, especially for kids and new fly casters. The casts don't need to be long, and panfish typically aren't too particular about the look of the fly.

The lightest, shortest fly rods and lines are all that's necessary for panfish; 2- and 4-weight rods and lines will do it. A floating line will be fine for fly casting to panfish, but if fish are holding at depth, use a weighted bead-head or put a few split shot on the leader.

For poppers, try size 10 to size 16 in black, white, red, or yellow. If sunfish hit a popper but you can't hook them, go down at least one size; 12 to 14, for example. Attractor patterns should include size 14 stimulators, hoppers, and crickets (deadly on calm summer ponds). Your box should also have small gnats, nymphs, and small Woolly Buggers to be fished in the surface film or subsurface.

For crappie-specific flies, consider minnow-imitating streamers in sizes 10 and 12 fished along the bottom. "Mini-jigs" can also be cast with a fly rod. Tie a single square knot in the upper leader section, or secure a bead there, and then slide the tippet and leader through a slip float. Tie on the mini-jig; it'll sink when cast, and the float will stop at the knot or bead for correct depth.

Catfish

Bullhead and White Catfish

Freshwater catfish occur all around the world. Bullheads (the smallest of the species) and white catfish can be fished with light tackle, while flatheads, channel, and blue catfish need some heftier gear.

With a typical maximum length of 12 to 15 inches, bullheads (whether black, brown, or yellow) are the most widespread, occurring in sluggish streams, ponds, and lakes across the country. They don't mind muddy water and can stand very warm water with low oxygen. Like other catfish, they can use their air bladders to breathe gaseous air in poor water conditions (they'll gulp air at the surface). A high, lobe-shaped dorsal fin and eight chin barbels are key identifying features. Depending upon their range, the three major bullhead species can closely resemble one another.

Bullheads are often present in the same waters where young anglers are casting for sunnies. They will bite during the day, but frequently tend to be more active at night. These fish hardly ever strike any sort of lure, so still-fishing with bait—natural or prepared—is pretty much standard.

White catfish are considered good eating (better than bullheads, certainly) and are frequently pursued for the table. They become active as water temperatures get into the 70s. They are identified by bluish-gray dorsal surfaces, a distinct edge between grayish flanks and white undersides, and a lack of spots. Matching the biggest yellow bullhead in size, white catfish can reach 18 inches and upwards of 3 pounds.

Techniques for Light-Tackle Catfish

For these smaller catfish, use light spinning or spincasting outfits loaded with 4- to 6-pound-test monofilament. Use as little weight as possible—just enough to get on the bottom. Set up a drop-shot rig with 12-inch hook leaders, or a rig with a sliding sinker pegged with a bead or split shot. Use long-shank size 4 to 2 hooks, and have pliers handy since bullheads tend to swallow baits, or use circle hooks.

Big bullheads and white catfish will take whole worms or minnows fished on the bottom, while a piece of night crawler hooked on a light jig head works for smaller fish. In early summer, crayfish also work. Leeches, strips of liver, and dough balls can also be effective. If fishing on the bottom with a relatively tight line, let the fish move off a distance before setting the hook. If keeping fish for eating, fish in relatively clear waters and put the fish on ice immediately.

Channel, Blue, and Flathead Catfish

Big catfish have a special place in American fishing history. Many a Midwesterner has tangled with a monster blue cat, and across many states, channel cats are a species of angling and eating delight.

Anglers find channel cats in rivers, creeks, and lakes across the entire country, and even into northern Mexico and southern Canada. They're

When you're targeting one of the bigger species of catfish, there's no telling just what kind of trophy you'll be dragging up out of the water. KEITH SUTTON

identified by their deeply forked, V-shaped tails with pointed lobes. Most range from 2 to 8 pounds. They prefer clear water and don't mind a little current.

Blue catfish are found in rivers and impoundments mostly across the South, as well as their original range in the Mississippi, Missouri, and Ohio Rivers. Blues have a deeply forked tail with rounded lobes, a body with no spots, and a longer anal fin and more rounded dorsal fin. Larger blue cats develop a bulky head and a distinct humped back at the base of the dorsal fin.

Flatheads like to go deep in tailraces below dams on big rivers, or in reservoirs and large tributaries. They can be found from western Pennsylvania across the Great Lakes drainages to the Dakotas and Idaho. They have a squared-off, slightly rounded tail and square-shaped dorsal fin; spade-shaped flat heads; and large, wide mouths.

Techniques for Big Catfish

Fishing from shore or at anchor and drift fishing from a boat are the main ways to pursue big catfish. Set lines (a heavy line with a single baited hook, tied to a tree) and trot lines (a length of line tied to a float, with several dropper hooks) are still used in some places to catch big cats.

In rivers, focus on tributary mouths, deep drop-offs, deeply undercut banks, and deep pools, especially pools with stumps, sunken logs, or boulders at the head. Channel cats are a bit more mobile than their larger brethren, and will move into shallows over gravel or rocky bottoms. Reservoir catfish take to deep flooded timber and to holes below inflowing tributaries.

Waters immediately below dams can be major catfish hideouts. Outflow from the dam creates a deep area of churning water, called a "scour hole," and

---

DOUGH BALLS

Seems like every avid catfisherman in the world has a private recipe for dough balls, something they swear by, a gooey glob that will catch fish when nothing else is working. As you become more experienced as a catfisher, doubtless you'll come up with your own recipes. But to make your basic, run-of-the-mill dough ball, put 1½ cups of cornmeal, 1 cup of flour, and 4 ounces of anise oil into a pot. Add 16 ounces of a sweet, fruit-flavored soft drink (non-diet) to the pot. Stir the mixture continuously over medium heat until all the fluid is absorbed and the dough is sticky and stiff. Put the mixture on a floured board and knead, adding more flour until the mix isn't sticky. Make grape-size balls and let cool before using.

A slip-float rig using ¼ ounce of large split shot, or a ¼-ounce slip sinker (egg sinker) baited with a big minnow, is very effective for locating channel cats in shallow water. A larger version of the slip-float rig with a heavier sinker and longer leader can go deep for bigger catfish. Use flat-sided sinkers with river rigs, as current will roll a round-sided sinker. ILLUSTRATION BY MICHAEL GELLATLY

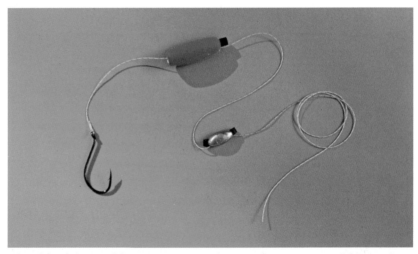

When fishing above soft bottoms in water without strong current, a small float on the leader keeps the bait just off the bottom. KEITH SUTTON

To make a river rig, pull a 50-pound-test superbraid through a three-way swivel. Tie a 24-inch 30-pound "big game" monofilament to the other barrel swivel eye, and snell this to a 6/0 octopus circle hook, possibly adding a swivel halfway down the leader. Tie a 5-ounce flat-sided or bell sinker to the third swivel eye using 20-pound monofilament. If the sinker or hook snags, the lighter monofilament will break before the main line does.
ILLUSTRATION BY MICHAEL GELLATLY

below this will be mounds of gravel and debris, pushed there by the outflow. Big blues and flatheads will station themselves in the hole, depending upon where churned-up baitfish spill out, and also seek the slower water behind debris mounds. Wing dams also attract catfish; the cats will patrol the downriver edge of the dam, depending on how deep the water is, and sometimes chase baitfish around to the upriver side. Make use of topographic charts, depth gauges, and sonar to locate holes and hiding spots and determine their size.

Tackle, Rigs, and Baits
Channel cats call for medium-action rods and reels—spincasting, spinning, or baitcasting—loaded with 10-pound-test line. For blue and flathead catfish, use heavy baitcasting rods and reels or conventional reels loaded with 30- to 50-pound-test line.

In terms of baits, channel cats will take anything from fish strips to crayfish to chicken liver, on size 2 to 1/0 hooks. For big blues and flatheads, try live or dead shiners or shad, strips of fish, and chicken livers, on size 3/0 to 5/0 hooks.

Trout

Everybody knows what you're talking about when you say "trout." But it turns out, the word can refer to quite a variety of fish. Brown trout are "true" trout, while brook trout, lake trout, and bull trout are actually char. Rainbow, cutthroat, and golden trout are grouped in the salmon genus. But all of these fish share very similar traits: lack of spines in their fins, an adipose fin (the small, thumb-like fin in front of the tail), and often very bright, highly detailed markings.

Rainbows are distinguished by the lengthwise pink or red stripe and the many small black spots on the fish's back and sides. They are found across the country, except for portions of the South.

American brown trout arose from introductions from Europe, with the first ones arriving from Germany in 1883. They have amber or silvery bodies with "coffee bean" black spots across their backs and red spots on their sides.

Brook trout have lower fins edged in white and irregular yellow blotches on their backs. They range from the Northeast into Canada, and down through the Appalachians into the mid-South; they have been introduced in the West.

There are fourteen different, identifiable variations within the cutthroat species. Most range up to 20 inches, with some fish breaking 4 pounds; coastal and lake-dwelling cutthroats get bigger. Cutthroats share their range with brown and rainbow trout, and hybridize with rainbows to make a "cutbow."

Cutthroat trout. SHUTTERSTOCK / DEC HOGAN

Brook trout. SHUTTERSTOCK / DAN THORNBERG

Brown trout. SHUTTERSTOCK / KLETR

Rainbow trout. SHUTTERSTOCK / ALEXANDER RATHS

OTHER MAJOR TROUT SPECIES

If you want to mix a little backpacking with your angling, seek the golden trout. This smaller but very pretty member of the salmonid family lives in lakes and headwaters at high elevation, mostly in the Sierras of California and a few other western states.

Another western species, the bull trout, is one of the bigger, more aggressive char. It is still endangered across much of its range in the Lower 48, but appears to be mounting a comeback in some waters.

The steelhead is a larger, oceangoing version of the rainbow trout, found in many western coastal rivers. This fish has also been established in the Great Lakes. Terrific and aggressive fighters, steelhead call anglers to the river in droves when they arrive to spawn.

The lake trout is a deep-dwelling char that can also take on some serious size and, in the northern cold-water lakes of Canada, becomes a vigorous fighter.

A beautiful Idaho steelhead. SHUTTERSTOCK / IDAK

Trout Techniques

Trout will readily take bait, including aquatic insects, worms, and leeches. Among artificial lures, trout anglers have been using in-line spinners and spoons since the late 1800s. When trout feed on the surface, they are almost always feeding on insects, which must be accurately imitated by flies.

In terms of tackle, for small-stream trout, an ultralight outfit works fine. Casting on rivers will take a medium-action spinning rod with some length, and spincasting and spinning reels loaded with up to 10-pount-test mono-filament work well. Going deep for big trout calls for medium to heavy rods, while steelhead require a long casting rod and spinning or conventional reel with strong drag.

Tackle, Rig, and Baits

Trout feed on baitfish (shiners, sculpins, and dace) and fall for plugs that cor-rectly imitate bait size and color. Plug fishing can be especially fruitful on big-ger creeks and rivers and in lakes. Most trout are ambush predators that strike quickly, so keep a plug moving and fish it through the entire strike zone.

Spinners usually don't need to be bigger than size 3 to take trout of all sizes. Small spoons are also fine, and need not get much bigger than 3 inches long. For live bait, rig a small minnow forward of the dorsal fin on a size 6 hook, and use a small casting sinker to get it on the bottom. A salmon egg on an egg hook or corn kernels or small worms on a size 8 hook, fished on the bottom, are also highly effective.

The culture of trout fishing is especially encouraging with regard to catch-and-release. Be sure to press your barbs flat so you can more easily let the fish loose unharmed.

Trout on the Fly

There are times when fly fishing is the only real way to approach a trout stream. When trout are keyed in on a mayfly, caddis, or stonefly hatch, other baits or lures will draw little interest. The key to using insect-imitating flies is to "match the hatch," which means to correctly identify the actual bugs that the trout are eating and reproduce them with your fly. Trout also readily eat larvae, or nymphs, that live along the stream bottom or drift or swim in the water column, and these, too, must be matched to what is in the angler's fly box. This is why you'll see fly fishers carrying several boxes bursting with flies—getting color and size correct is crucial.

Streamers can also be highly effective, given how much trout feed on forage fish. Try a "dead-drift" (letting the fly float freely along, feathers and other materi-als fluttering in the current) or strip it in, making it dart like a fleeing baitfish.

Dry Flies

Trout will occasionally focus on a hatching insect so sharply that they will pass up other bugs. As a hatch fades, however, casting a dry fly of a different species will often trigger a trout strike. When there is no visible hatch of insects, cast nymph patterns that mimic the local species.

Dry flies are meant to imitate actual insects. These four variations on a caddis fly, left, are intended to imitate the natural fly, right.

Streamers

Drift streamers across the current so that trout see the full profile of the fly, suggesting a struggling baitfish. On a dead-drift with a streamer, trout often hit it on the "swing" at the end of the drift as the streamer turns a tight arc. When stripping a streamer, pull it in with short, darting strips of the line, pausing between each strip.

Nymph Patterns

In moving water, cast nymphs upstream, mend your line, then let the nymph dead-drift along. Depending on the water depth and the temperament of the fish (heavily fished trout will often spook more readily), position a strike indicator 7 or 8 feet up your leader. More experienced anglers will sometimes forego the strike indicator, but beginners should almost always use one. In tailwaters and other consistent streams of a predictable flow rate and depth, the strike indicator will often be used as a float, suspending the nymph at a certain level in the water.

Nymphs can be tied off the bottom of a heavier fly (a Woolly Bugger or a streamer, for instance) and can also be tied off the bottom of a buoyant dry fly, something like a grasshopper.

Muskie, Pike, and Pickerel

The members of the pike family look like they were designed to cause trouble. Their torpedo-shaped bodies and sharp, flat snouts, their greenish sides and mouths full of teeth . . . It all says, "Don't mess with me." But you should, you should.

Pike and pickerel are often willing quarry. Pike can be very curious and will often follow a lure some distance before striking. Other times, both pickerel and pike make sudden, slashing strikes at lures. Muskies, or muskellunge, are a good bit more difficult to catch, especially larger, smarter fish.

Pickerel are found all through the Northeast to Florida, and up from Louisiana to the Midwest and into Canada. They have dark horizontal markings like a series of chains down their olive sides, as well as a black vertical patch under each eye. Most chain pickerel are around 2 pounds and not much more than 25 or 30 inches long. Two smaller subspecies, the grass pickerel and redfin pickerel, have dark vertical markings on their sides.

Pickerel and pike overlap a good deal across their range, and both species take to similar environments. But pickerel will often be closer to shore, in the

SHUTTERSTOCK / MATT HOWARD

SHUTTERSTOCK / BARRY BLACKBURN

While very similar in appearance, and while chain pickerel (bottom) and northern pike (top) will often overlap ranges, they prefer different environments and water temperatures.

most shallow weed and lily pad sections, while pike prefer weedy structure in 5 to 6 feet of water to depths of 12 feet or more, and water temperatures from the mid-50s into the 60s. Pike inhabit cold waters across the Northeast and upper Midwest, in the Great Lake states, and across the Northwest and much of Canada. They have strong green-colored sides marked with white, horizontal, bean-shaped spots and often have orange-tinted, heavily marked fins.

Muskies are native to the Great Lakes and upper Mississippi drainages, as far west as Iowa, and occurring in the southern Appalachians. They have light-green sides with vertical striations, unlike the horizontal markings of pike and pickerel.

Fishing for Pickerel and Pike

Bright, flashy spoons, spinnerbaits, plugs, and in-line spinners are go-to lures for pickerel. Live-rigged baitfish, mainly shiners, minnows, or small suckers, are an ideal bait, hooked through the base of the dorsal fin. In colder weather, focus on fallen trees and submerged brush, and slow down your retrieve of small crankbaits or soft-plastic jerkbaits.

Pike in lakes seek thick, vegetative cover around drop-offs, inlet mouths, and deeper coves and bays. In rivers, pike occupy slower and slack water in current seams, below points and islands, and below docks and dams. In a lure, look for a combination of bright colors, metallic flash, and noise. Fish shallow-running plugs and crankbaits over weeds, diving plugs along drop-offs, and spinnerbaits around brush and logs. Try spoons and in-line spinners fished along weed beds, or work white or silver jigs and swimbaits along the deepest weedy points. To guard against pike teeth, use a light, nylon-coated wire leader; big pike call for heavier braided-wire leaders.

When it comes to picking out a pike lure, don't be bashful about size or color. DAVID DIRKS

Fly Fishing for Pike

Fly fishing for pike can be excellent in weedy shallows where wading or casting from a boat is possible. Tippets should be rated to at least 12 pounds. Use 15 inches of 30-pound nylon-coated wire as a bite guard. A fly rod for pike should be at least an 8-weight. Cast divers and poppers on a floating line to shallow pike, or big streamers on slow-sinking lines.

Fishing for Muskie

To fish for muskie well requires a boat and lots of room for lure storage. Some commercially produced lures reach 12 or 14 inches in length and include large bucktail spinners, swimbaits, and soft plastics. Much like pike, muskies are attracted to brightness, flash, and high-contrast patterns.

Muskies are notoriously difficult to catch and are often called the "fish of 10,000 casts." PHOTO OBTAINED/ACQUIRED FROM OHIO DEPARTMENT OF NATURAL RESOURCES, DIVISION OF WILDLIFE WEBSITE, WWW.WILDOHIO.COM

Use stout, 6- to 8-foot baitcasting rods and conventional reels loaded with at least 20-pound test, monofilament or braided. Seven-strand wire leaders from 80- to 100-pound test are also standard.

Muskies will range from shallow to deep water and rove along at depths of 30 feet or more, especially in summer. Tributary mouths, seams of current, and drop-offs to deep water behind islands and rocks are muskie hangouts. Muskies will set up ambushes in patches of timber, in submerged channels, or over bars and shoals on the bottom. Weeds at the edge of deep water or drop-offs, and floating weeds or vegetation are preferred hideouts.

Fishing from a boat, start out shallow with jerkbaits or spinnerbaits, and if nothing happens, start working down with crankbaits. Experiment with bucktails of different sizes and colors, with different blade shapes. Fish high-contrast-patterned diving plugs over and into deep vegetation and along drop-offs. Always work your lure in a figure-eight pattern at the boat if you see or suspect a muskie is following.

Fly Fishing for Muskie

Few people fly fish for muskie, but it can be done with 10- or 11-weight, fast-action rods and 10- to 15-inch flies. Target post-spawn muskies in creek mouths, weedy coves, and shallow bays. Use snakelike rabbit-fur flies (divers, usually) in color combinations of white, green, chartreuse, black, and pink. Retrieve the fly with a continuous, quick hand-strip; if there are no strikes, change flies or put on a sink-tip and go deeper.

Walleye and Sauger

Inhabiting clear lakes and slower rivers throughout the Great Lakes region, the West, and the Northeast, walleyes draw anglers much the same way the largemouth does in the South. The sauger is the walleye's smaller but very similar cousin, sometimes called "sand pike."

Most walleyes are a gold-olive color, with a dark green dorsal surface and head and white belly. Specific identifiers for walleye are a reflective eye (often with a white appearance), a dark mark at the rear base of the first dorsal fin, and a white-tipped lower tail-fin lobe. Walleyes usually have elongated, paddle-shaped bodies, with a high, sharp, spine-tipped first dorsal fin.

Walleyes prefer clearer waters with rocky, sandy, or gravel bottoms in the open sections of reservoirs or lakes. Often walleyes can be found congregating near reefs and shoals, over rock piles, or along weedy sections. Water temperatures from the mid-60s to the upper 70s are best. They're frequently found in schools, especially during the late spring or early summer spawn.

A walleye. SHUTTERSTOCK / DAN THORNBERG

Looking like a small walleye, saugers have black spots on their first dorsal fin, lack the white-tipped tail lobe, and have scaled cheeks. Saugers vary from brownish olive to a gray-brown with yellowish highlights and a white belly. They range through the Great Lakes states, south through the Appalachians to Tennessee, and west to Montana. Most saugers don't break 14 inches, with larger fish hitting 20 inches.

Saugers will tolerate water much more turbid than walleyes, and have been introduced farther south. Shallow lakes and slow rivers with silty or turbid water ranging in temperature from the low 60s to mid-70s are the preferred habitat. They spend more time on the bottom than walleyes, and stay deeper more often. Keeping in mind these differences in turbidity, temperature, and habitat preferences, many of the same fishing techniques that work for walleye will also often work for sauger.

The Walleye Bite

Walleye follow baitfish. Sometimes that means they're in slower sections of a river, or maybe the big, open waters of a deep lake. If walleyes aren't chasing baitfish, they're hanging around structure anticipating the baitfish. They do so in schools, and that's to the angler's advantage: Where you catch one walleye, there should be more. Casting and retrieving, drift-fishing, and trolling various baits and lures are all productive.

Walleyes don't have a very strong strike, and often give several taps on a natural bait or lure during the retrieve before they start pulling. They'll eat shiners, shad, minnows, perch, alewives (a baitfish similar to shad), and crayfish, and this diet dictates lure and bait choices. Saugers tend to eat the same sort of things, but strike baits more aggressively than walleyes.

Spinning and baitcasting outfits are the main walleye tackle. Either of these can be used for trolling, though baitcasting or conventional reels

Walleye (and sauger) are famously the tastiest fish in freshwater. Their flesh is light, flaky, and flavorful. If they're biting, most anglers will keep as many as regulations will allow.
SHUTTERSTOCK / DAN THORNBERG

are easier to use on big, deep water. Rod length varies from 6 to 7 feet and doesn't need to be longer, except when trolling deep. Monofilament or super-lines work fine, in 6- to 12-pound test.

Trolling for Walleye

When walleyes are deep, probing with sonar or trolling lures at differing depths is the main way to locate them. Most walleye trolling is done at around 2 miles per hour or less, just enough speed to create proper lure action. Spoons, plugs, and beaded in-line spinner-blade harnesses for worms or minnows work for trolling. In the summer, the largest walleyes often patrol the open waters of big lakes, chasing baitfish.

Lures and Baits

Cast diving crankbaits, jerkbaits and minnows, blade baits, spoons, spinnerbaits, and tube baits to walleye and sauger hangouts. In the fall, walleyes and saugers in lakes congregate on structure, where they can be targeted with cast-and-retrieve lures. Walleyes in rivers most often hug the deepest water along cuts and structure, and bottom-seeking lures work best. A live minnow or small jig with a grub or worm can drift below a slip float through easy river current or over lake structure.

Lindy Rigs

Lindy Rigs baited with minnows, worms, or leeches can be still-fished, drifted, or slow-trolled. The sliding-sinker configuration on most Lindy Rigs lets wall-eye take the bait without feeling much resistance from the sinker. Bait Lindy Rigs by hooking a minnow through the lip, a night crawler through the nose or collar, or a leech behind its mouth.

Jigs

Walleye and saugers both nail jigs, but keeping the jig vertical and on the bottom (use enough weight) are key. Hair jigs or grub-tailed jigs from ¼ to ½ ounce with round lead heads are good choices; go with light colors in clear water and orange in silty water. Target deep spots along riprap, below wing dams, and in the tailwaters immediately below main dams.

Atlantic Salmon

Atlantic salmon are still a major quarry in eastern Canadian waters (as well as Scandinavia, northern Europe, Scotland, Ireland, and Russia). Once prolific in coastal rivers from Maine to Connecticut, in North America they are now found mostly in Quebec, Newfoundland, New Brunswick, and Nova Scotia.

The Atlantic salmon and the brown trout are closely related. When spawning, the Atlantic salmon can look like a big, bullish brown trout, taking on a buttery yellow or caramel color with numerous reddish and black

Atlantic salmon. SHUTTERSTOCK / EDWARD WESTMACOTT

splotches on their sides. At sea, Atlantic salmon have a bluish back and silvery sides with small black splotches, and adults have a squared-off tail fin. Most Atlantic salmon run from 10 to 20 pounds, but older fish—up to eight years old—can get much larger.

Spawning Atlantic Salmon

Just like Pacific salmon, the Atlantic salmon is pursued on its spawning run, but this salmon will pass on fly after fly; make endless, speedy runs when hooked; and often leap clear of the water. Bringing an Atlantic salmon to the net is a significant angling achievement.

Spawning Atlantic salmon enter rivers in the late spring and fall, but don't immediately move upriver. The spawn is not complete until late fall or early winter, and the fish can either then return to the sea or overwinter in the river. Atlantic salmon do not die after a first spawning and can return to spawn two or three times. The biggest salmon usually return to freshwater the earliest and are capable of multiple spawning runs over their lifetime.

Atlantic Salmon Techniques

An Atlantic salmon might look at your fly on the first cast, lunge for it, miss, and mysteriously never make a move toward it again. Hence, dozens and dozens of fly patterns have been invented to induce the Atlantic salmon to grab and hold on. In some places in Canada and Europe, various metal lures are used, but in general, anglers fly fish for Atlantic salmon.

These fish frequently inhabit the deeper sections of large rivers and can sprint at high speed over significant distances, frequently going airborne at the end of a run. The fly fisher will need a 9- or 10-weight, 9- or 10-foot rod to make the necessary distance casts. Sinking and floating fly lines can both be deployed, depending on fly choice, but the reel should be loaded with as much backing as possible. A standard fly rod with a fighting butt is a good idea. For those inclined, a two-handed Spey rod can help reach far sections of a big river, but the casting technique for these big sticks is an art all its own.

Atlantic salmon anglers will see both "early fish" that come in the spring and "late fish" that come upriver in the fall. The salmon will travel along the bottom in freshwater, hugging the gravel in both shallow and deep sections. Occasionally anglers will be able to sight-cast to resting Atlantic salmon, sometimes finding them along the edge of the river. Most often, though, casting flies to long, deep pools and swinging flies through the current is the way to prospect for fish.

Traditional salmon flies are intended to trigger a salmon's strike with bright, flashy colors and high profile. Drift the fly sideways to the current to

Spawning Atlantic salmon will enter rivers in the late spring and fall, but won't start their migration upstream right away. SHUTTERSTOCK / MARK CAUNT

present the full profile to the fish. Salmon often hit the fly on the "swing" as the fly comes around in the current at the end of a cast. Anglers work the tops, deep sections, and tails of pools where Atlantic salmon collect, swinging flies directly to them. Atlantic salmon are not actually eating anything on their spawn run but "react" to various flies out of instinctive reflex.

Landlocked Salmon

The landlocked salmon is a version of the Atlantic salmon that lives entirely in freshwater, in both lakes and rivers in New England and eastern Canada. They dwell in the deeper sections of lakes, living on baitfish, and move up creeks to spawn. Landlocked salmon typically range from 3 to 8 pounds and have also been introduced to Lake Ontario and Lake Michigan, resulting in some big specimens.

Fishing for landlocked salmon often involves trolling flies through varying sections of deep lakes. Springtime trolling covers shallows after ice-out to mid-depths, and then the fish drop down to the coldest water in early summer. Fly-rod trolling setups involve 9-foot, 8- or 9-weight rods with 20-foot leaders on sinking lines; reels should have sufficient backing. Trolling flies for landlocked salmon are most often streamers that imitate smelt, a silvery-amber, 4- to 7-inch-long baitfish.

Pacific Salmon

While they might require some travel for most anglers, the biggest species of Pacific salmon—chinook (king), coho (silver), and sockeye—are worth the trek to the West Coast and Alaska. Strong, fierce, and determined fighters, these species offer great battles on medium to heavy tackle.

In their sea-dwelling chrome-colored phase, Pacific salmon are excellent food fish. But once they begin to take on their spawning colors, their edibility drops quickly. All Pacific species of salmon die after their single spawning run to their birth waters; in many places, salmon in full-spawn colors are off-limits to angling. Chinook, coho, kokanee sockeye, and pink salmon have been introduced to the Great Lakes.

The most well-known Pacific salmon by sight is the sockeye, often depicted in its brick-red spawning colors, its head a bright green. However, chinook salmon are often found in supermarkets and are thus known for their edibility (though the sockeye, with its high oil content, is probably the best eating of all).

Chinook Salmon
The chinook salmon is the largest of the Pacific salmon, easily reaching 50 pounds. Before spawning, chinooks have silvery bodies, with bluish backs and black spots above the lateral line, and lightly spotted fins. A key identifier of the chinook is its entirely black mouth, with black jaws and gums.

Sockeye Salmon
Sockeye salmon spawn only in coastal rivers that lead to a lake, where they assemble for their final move upstream. At sea and early in the spawning run, sockeyes have greenish backs and silvery sides, with very few dark spots or speckles. Most sockeyes average 6 to 8 pounds, with a few breaking 10 pounds. A smaller, landlocked version of the sockeye, called the kokanee, dwell in numerous western lakes.

Coho Salmon
A bit larger than the sockeye, the coho is a spectacular fighter, often leaping clear of the water. Coho salmon in their pre-spawn phase have bluish-green backs, silver sides, and black spots over their backs. In spawning colors, cohos take on pinkish-red sides with black-green, heavily spotted backs and greatly curved jaw kypes.

A chinook, or king, salmon. SHUTTERSTOCK / DEEPSPACEDAVE

A spawning-phase sockeye. SHUTTERSTOCK / IRYNA HARRY

Coho salmon are famously great fighters. SHUTTERSTOCK / KEITH PUBLICOVER

Pink Salmon

The pink salmon, the smallest Pacific species, lives for only two years, whereas other species live for four. Spawning males develop a humped back in front of the dorsal fin, resulting in the nickname "humpbacked salmon," or "humpie." At sea, pink salmon have a bluish back with black spots and silver sides; spawning colors are brownish olive, and the males have a pink-red stripe.

Catching Pacific Salmon

Methods for taking Pacific species are more wide open than tactics for Atlantic spawn-run salmon. From Northern California to the Kenai Peninsula, anglers head out to inshore waters, bays, and estuaries to catch chinook and coho salmon as they approach coastal rivers. Trolling and drifting natural baits and lures, jigging, back-trolling or "mooching," and trolling Pacific-style salmon flies are all employed. Anglers using downriggers nab the big kings in Puget Sound just as they do on Lake Ontario.

Salmon-egg sacks drifted just off the bottom, with a float above the hook, nab chinooks in coastal rivers in summer. A variety of bright spoons and spinners cast from the bank will take cohos and sockeyes in rivers. Deep-running, crankbait-like lures, capable of fast wiggles or flutters, induce chinook strikes on numerous western and Alaska rivers. When bank fishing for chinooks, check the terrain downstream to be sure you can run after a hooked fish.

Great Lakes Salmon

The better Great Lakes coho fisheries are in Lake Michigan and Lake Superior. Great Lakes chinooks and cohos moving up tributaries are best pursued close to the lake, as their strike reflex fades the farther they go upstream. Trolling for Great Lakes coho runs from late winter through fall, and chinook from summer through fall. Many of the same spoons, plugs, and baits used on the West Coast can also be successful in the Great Lakes.

Tackle

Chinook salmon are often color-selective and will often prefer to strike a lure of a specific color. Chinook call for heavy spinning tackle or conventional tackle, with line rated to 40 pounds. Sockeyes and cohos can be taken with medium-weight spinning or conventional tackle with a good drag system and a minimum of 15-pound-test line.

Pacific Salmon on Flies

The two main Pacific salmon species taken on the fly are coho and sockeye, but a fly caster who puts the right fly in front of a river-running fish could take

A salmon-trolling rig, complete with (raised) outriggers. SHUTTERSTOCK / VERA BOGAERTS

any Pacific salmon. Cohos, like Atlantic salmon, leap high and often when in freshwater. Sockeyes are excellent game fish on medium-weight rods, and often swim shallow enough for sight-casting. Pink and chum salmon can also be taken on the fly, usually incidentally when anglers aim for coho and sockeye. Chinook salmon sometimes take flies, but are such big fish that they call for 10- or 11-weight rods. Anglers casting flies to cohos often tangle with chinooks.

Flies for sockeye and coho can be as simple as a piece of green or hot-pink yarn on a red 2/0 hook. "Chromers," or salmon running early from the ocean or lake, will still strike actively at bright, bothersome targets. Various patterns in pink, silver, white, bright orange, and green, bead-head or not, will bring strikes. Chinook salmon can be taken on flies that combine bright or fluorescent pink, green, and red combined with black or purple. The more a salmon cues on color, the less it will accurately strike, and thus many fish caught "in color" are foul-hooked.

Epoxy flies tied with dumbbell heads and bead-head flies have enough weight to get down in shallow water if cast with floating line. Day-Glo egg, roe, and egg-sucking leech patterns can produce for Pacific salmon. Bead-head

CHOOSING A GUIDE

No matter what kind of fish you're going after, whether it's trout in Montana, salmon in Alaska, bass in Florida, or pike in Saskatchewan, there's going to be someone out there who knows how to do it better than you do, and is willing to share his or her expertise and knowledge for a (relatively small) daily fee. When the alternative is a day stumbling around blind, fishing the wrong lures in the wrong spots, wasting time, it's hard to think of a better way to spend three or four hundred dollars than with a fishing guide.

If you're unfamiliar with an area and you don't have personal recommendations for a guide, your first call should be to one of the area's reputable fishing shops. A quick Web search will come up with the listings. Tell them you're new to the area, give them a description of your skill level (beginner, intermediate, etc.), and tell them you're looking for a guide. If they're an outfitter as well as a retail outlet, they'll charge a small fee for acting as intermediary.

Be sure to call well ahead, though. The best fishing guides in the most desirable areas can often book up months in advance.

"comet" flies look like big dry flies but come in Day-Glo and metallic colors. Depending upon water depth and current, anglers should use a sink-tip line.

Fly presentations to Pacific salmon are almost always done on or just above the bottom. When sight-casting to salmon, cast upstream and drift the fly horizontally to the current and into the noses of the salmon. Similar to swinging a fly to (unseen) Atlantic salmon, Pacific species will often grab a fly on the end of its drift.

Chapter Six

Essential Fishing Knots

Given the repeated necessity of tying flies or lures onto your line (several times during a morning of fishing), and of tying leader to line, there are a handful of specialized knots with which most anglers need to be proficient. Before going out onto the water, spend a morning at home practicing these knots, repeating them until your hands have gained a certain amount of muscle memory and you feel confident that you can repeat the action outside on a windy day. The right knot in the right situation will make you a better angler and save you all kinds of frustration.

A couple things to remember: Before tightening any knot, be sure to moisten the line, either with spittle or by dipping it in the stream. The friction of tightening the line can potentially create enough heat to melt the line, compromising the integrity of the knot. And after tying any knot, test it by pulling firmly in opposing directions. You don't have to jerk it hard. Just a steady, strong pull. It's much better to learn about a weak knot *before* you hook a fish.

The Improved Clinch

For attaching line and leader to swivels, sinkers, or terminal tackle (lures, flies), the improved clinch knot is perhaps the most common knot in fishing, and works fine with monofilament line up to 20-pound test. The breaking strength of this knot, when tied properly, is close to 95 percent. (It's not, however, the best knot to tie with braided lines.)

This knot locks against the hook eye or split ring, which means that for those lures that need a lot of swimming action, the improved clinch can prove too restricting. And while it works well for small flies tied to 6X or 7X tippets, be careful that the knot's rigidity doesn't put the flies at an odd angle.

Vary the number of wraps depending upon the diameter of the monofilament. For 4- to 8-pound test, six wraps work fine. Five wraps suffice for 8- to 16-pound test. Above 20-pound test, wrap the tag end three or four times around the standing line. Always make sure the wraps tighten evenly, without overlapping, and that the tag end is secured against the split ring under the wraps.

Steps:

1. Pass the tag end through the split ring of the lure, and bring it back up along the standing line.
2. Make four to six wraps around the standing line with the tag end; space these evenly and don't try to make them tightly.

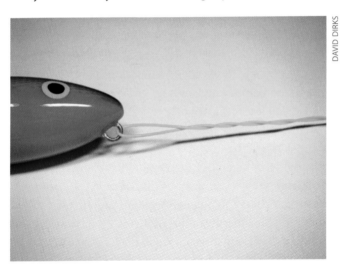

3. Pass the tag end through the loop between the split ring and the first wrap.

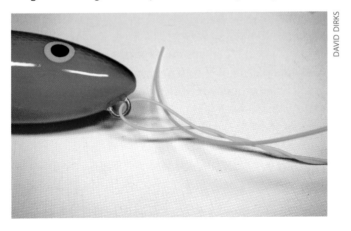

3. Pass the tag end through the loop just created by the descending tag end and the standing line.

4. Pull and hold on to the tag end, and then pull on the standing line, pulling away from the lure.

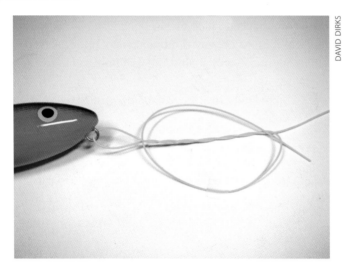

5. Tighten the knot by pulling on both the standing line and tag end; the wraps should stack up and cinch. Press down on the wraps to even them if need be.

6. Clip the tag end very close to the knot.

The Palomar Knot

The Palomar knot is an alternative to the improved clinch for securing terminal tackle, and unlike the improved clinch, works well with braided lines. It is also good for tying tippets to flies that need a lot of action; the Palomar knot is smaller than the improved clinch and thus affects the fly's movement less. It works well with monofilament up to 20-pound test, but not much beyond. The thickness and stiffness of heavier monofilament often won't allow the knot to cinch tightly and evenly against the split ring, and most likely the knot will come loose.

The basic Palomar knot provides 90 to 95 percent breaking strength with monofilament.

Steps:

1. Pass the bight through the hook eye so that you have 6 to 8 inches on the other side.

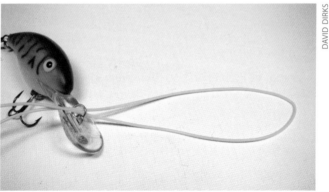

2. Bend the bight back around, crossing the standing line, and make a single overhand knot with the bight and line. Open up the bight so that you have a lasso-like loop.

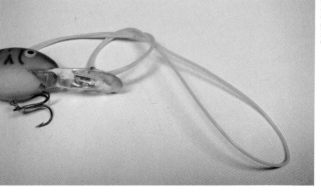

3. Pass the body of the lure or fly through this loop; the bight section needs to be long enough to accommodate the whole lure.

4. Get the lure through the loop, and then just let it hang again from the line.

DAVID DIRKS

5. With the lure through the loop, moisten the knot, and pull on the standing line and on the bight end.

6. Cinch the knot into a small fist shape and cut the bight end closely (both strands).

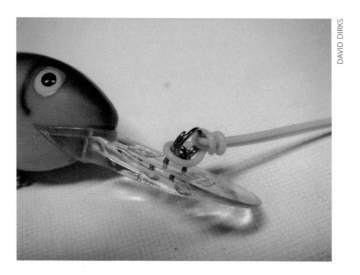

DAVID DIRKS

The Non-slip Loop Knot

Similar to the improved clinch, the non-slip loop knot creates a small, fixed loop that doesn't cinch against the hook eye or split ring, and therefore puts zero direct tension on the lure. This helps maximize the lure's darting, wiggling, or swimming action in the water. This knot is also a very good choice for weighted flies, as it lets them fall freely through the water, putting full emphasis on the wavy, lifelike effect of various fly materials and feathers.

The main objective when tying this knot is to get the loop right. A loop that's a bit bigger than it should be isn't a major problem, but no loop in any test line should be wider than half the lure width; otherwise, it can act as a baffle in front of the lure, affecting the performance. Loops in front of flies can be pretty small, as long as they let the fly swim freely.

Use this knot with plugs and jerkbaits and with lures that need to wobble, like certain kinds of spoons. It's also right for big flies like bass bugs and bulky streamers. It has about a 70 percent breaking strength when tied correctly, but as you fish with it, check the terminal loop now and then to make sure it hasn't been nicked or abraded.

Steps:

1. Tie a single, loose overhand knot in the standing line, and then pass the tag end through the lure's split ring.

2. Pass the tag end through the main loop of the overhand knot, but don't tighten.

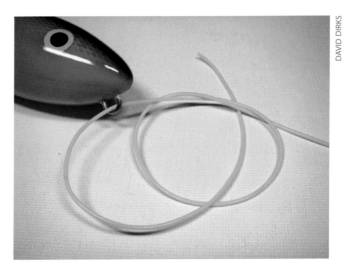

DAVID DIRKS

3. Wrap the tag end around the standing line, just like in a clinch knot.

4. The test-line strength determines how many wraps you make around the standing line above the knot. For monofilament up to 10-pound test, make seven wraps; for 10- to 14-pound test, make five wraps. Four wraps will suffice for monofilament from 16- to 40-pound test. Over 40-pound test, make three wraps.

5. Complete the wraps, and slip the tag end through the overhand knot, going in the opposite direction that it came through.

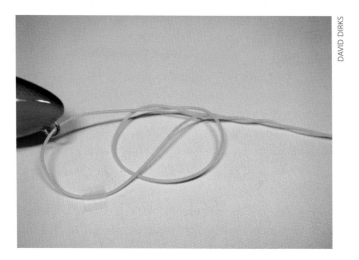

DAVID DIRKS

6. Pull a short length of the tag end through the overhand knot loop toward the lure.

7. Pull evenly on the standing line and the tag end to close the overhand knot and snug up the wraps, cinching the tag end.

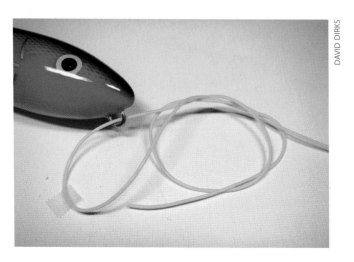

DAVID DIRKS

8. To finish the knot, pull on the loop and the tag end, seating the wraps tightly and securing the whole knot.

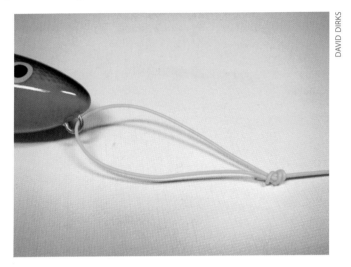

DAVID DIRKS

The Surgeon's Knot

This is an easy way to join lighter monofilaments of similar diameter. It works well in a variety of situations, as in cold weather with stiff fingers and stiffened line. It also works with monofilament, fluorocarbon, and braided lines, although when tied with braided line, it has to be carefully tightened to make sure the tucks bind and seat evenly.

The surgeon's knot is popular among fly fishers because it serves well as a connection between the leader and the tippet. In a pinch, it can also be used to make fly leaders, connecting the various sections of the leader, but blood knots usually make that connection. Tied properly, the surgeon's knot has breaking strength in the 95 percent range. It works best with lines up to 12-pound test.

Steps:

1. Bring together and overlap 6 or 8 inches of each line to be joined, pinching them in place. These overlapping lines should be reasonably close in diameter and strength; one shouldn't be significantly thicker than the other.

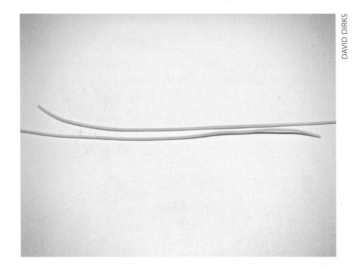

2. Make a loop with the overlapping sections, pinch it, and then tuck one tag end and the entire length of the other line through.

3. Repeat the tuck, again bringing one tag end and the entire length of the other line through the loop. Be sure to keep the loop and first tuck pinched together, and don't let them slip as you make the second tuck.

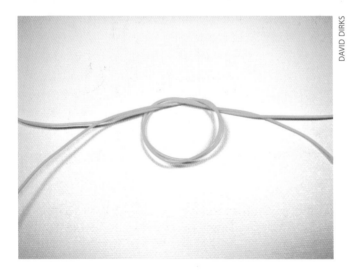

4. Make a third and final tuck with the one tag end and the other entire line or with the whole tippet.

5. You should have what amounts to a triple overhand knot, ready to be tightened, with the loop made by both strands still slightly open.

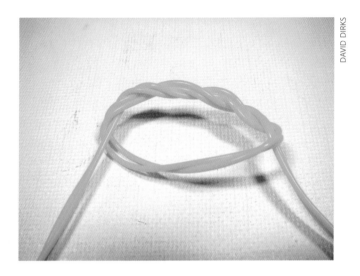

6. Hold both lines and both tag ends in either hand (a tag end and a standing line in either hand) and pull evenly to tighten.

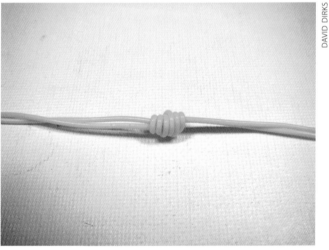

The Blood Knot

Fly fishers frequently use blood knots to construct tapered leaders and to link descending sections of monofilament from the butt section to the tippet. The ensuing series of blood knots creates a leader that unfurls naturally, without kinking or being misshaped. Blood knots are also useful in constructing rigs or connecting leaders to the main line.

This knot is best used for tying together strands of monofilament that are the same or close in diameter (hence its use in creating a leader with a tapering diameter). The blood knot isn't a knot that works well with most braided lines, or to join monofilament to braided line.

Steps:

1. Overlap 5 to 6 inches of the two lines to get the knot started. You'll need one hand to hold the lines together and the other hand to make the wraps with the tag end.

2. Don't twirl together the tag end and the line around which you're wrapping it—that will create unwanted twists. Wrap the first tag end in even turns around the other line without twisting that standing line.

3. With 2- to 12-pound-test line, make five wraps with each tag end around each standing line. With line up to 20-pound test, make three or four wraps.

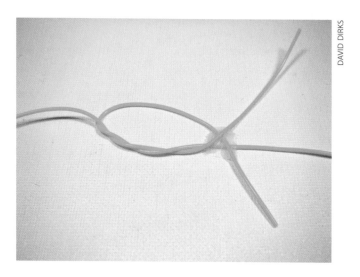

4. With the first set of wraps completed, bring the tag end back and down between the two lines, pinching it in place.

5. Wrap the other tag end around the opposite standing line, and bring the tag end through the center loop in the opposite direction of the first tag end.

DAVID DIRKS

6. Pull on both tag ends—one going up, one going down—to bring the wraps together and seat them snugly.

7. Use each hand to hold each standing line, using the fingers of each hand to pull on the tag ends.

DAVID DIRKS

8. With the wraps seated, pull smoothly on the standing lines to close and cinch the knot completely.

9. You should have an even, barrel-shaped knot with the tag ends above and below; trim the tag ends even with the wraps.

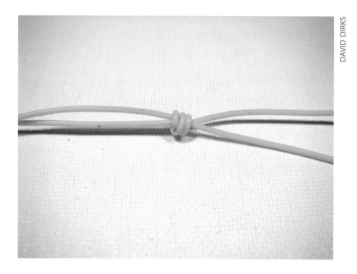

DAVID DIRKS

Adding a Dropper Fly

For fly fishing, you can extend a length of line from a blood knot for tying on a second, or "dropper," fly close to the bottom of the leader. Employ up to 12 inches of one line instead of the usual 5 or 6 inches of overlapping line in Step 1. As you finish the wraps, draw this extra-long tag-end length through the center loop. When you close the knot, this dropper extension will come directly from the knot center.

The Tube (or Nail) Knot

Most people shake their heads when they first encounter the tube knot, or nail knot, because they see a bunch of coils and some kind of implement—a nail, drinking straw, or stick—and they're intimidated. But this is an easy knot to tie and a great one to know, especially for fly fishers who need a strong knot to attach a leader butt end to the end of the main fly line, or to attach backing to the end of the fly line.

The tube knot is useful in affixing a smaller-diameter line to a larger-diameter line. Monofilament, backing line, and braided line affixed to a fly line all do just that: cinch really tightly. You can tie this knot with a section of a plastic drinking straw, the body of a ballpoint pen, a knitting needle, or a nail—anything that helps make a tunnel of wrapped line.

This knot in its doubled form can work with monofilament; a single nail knot between strands of monofilament can slide and give way. When the wraps close evenly, this knot can tightly secure a braided line to another braided line.

Steps:

1. Overlap the thin and thick lines, with the thinner line coming from the left (for right-handers).

1. Place the section of tube against both lines, and pinch the thin and thick lines and the tube together with your left hand.

2. Wrap the tag end of the thin line around both lines and the tube, moving from right to left.

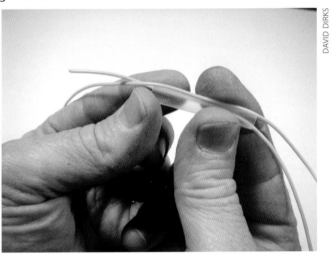

DAVID DIRKS

3. Create a series of five or six wraps around both lines and the tube, holding them in place with your left fingers.

4. After the final wrap, insert the tag end of the thin line into the tube and bring it out the other open end.

5. Pinch the wraps lightly with your left thumb and forefinger, and with your right hand slip the tube out from under your left fingers and the wraps.

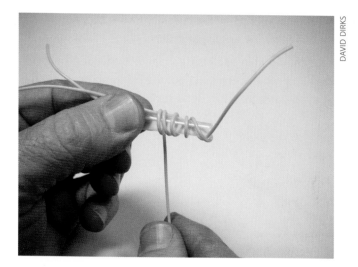

6. Pull the tube completely off the thin line.

7. Hold the assembly of wraps lightly in your fingers, and pull steadily on the tag end of the thin line.

8. Pulling the tag end will cinch the wraps around the two lines; do this slowly, watching to be sure each wrap tightens evenly.

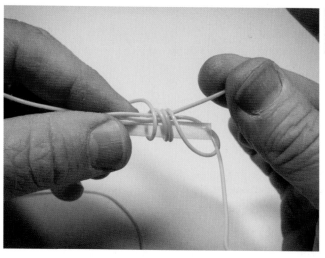

9. Pull on the main section of thin line and the tag end, and then pull on the thin line and thick line simultaneously.

10. The wraps should sit in a solid, fist-shaped, even-sided knot with the thin line extending without any kinks out the bottom. Trim the tag ends close enough to the knot that they don't stick out.

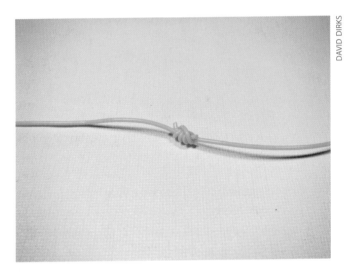

DAVID DIRKS

Double Tube Knot

A double tube knot can be used to secure two lines of the same or similar diameter.

Steps:

1. Overlap a significant length of the two lines, and then tie but don't tighten one tube knot with one tag end.

2. Tie a second tube knot with the other tag end on the other standing line, and don't tighten it.

3. Pull the standing lines to unite the knots, and then pull on the tag ends and standing lines to cinch them completely.

Appendix A
Conservation

Any guidebook that deals with fishing has to, at some point, discuss conservation. It's self-evident that the only way we can continue to fish is if there are *places* to fish. Conservation and environmentalism are too often politicized, but there's nothing overtly political about preserving the waters you love.

Fortunately, there are a number of organizations out there that are fighting the good fight. As an angler, the first check you write should go toward a rod and reel, lures, and waders. But the second check—after you come home from a day on the water, sunburned and tired, exhausted but somehow rejuvenated, replaying the day's best take and biggest fish—should be a donation to those organizations that have worked so hard, and *continue* to work hard, to make sure the water and fish are there for you to enjoy.

American Rivers
444 N. Capitol St. NW, Ste. 725
Washington, DC 20005
www.americanrivers.org

Atlantic Salmon Federation
PO Box 5200
St. Andrews, NB Canada E5B 3S8
(506) 529-1056
www.asf.ca

Izaak Walton League of America
707 Conservation Ln.
Gaithersburg, MD 202878
(301) 548-0150
www.iwla.org

National Fish and Wildlife Foundation
1133 15th St. NW
Washington, DC 20005
(202) 857-0166
www.nfwf.org

Nature Conservancy
4245 N. Fairfax Dr., Ste. 100
Arlington, VA 22203
(703) 841-5300
www.nature.org

Save Our Wild Salmon
200 1st Ave. W, Ste. 101
Seattle, WA 98119
(206) 286-4455
www.wildsalmon.org

Trout Unlimited
1300 N. 17th St.
Arlington, VA 22209
(800) 834-2419
www.tu.org

Western Native Trout Initiative
31664 Snowshoe Rd.
Evergreen, CO 80439
(303) 236-4402
www.westernnativetrout.org

Wild Fish Conservancy
15629 Main St. NE
Duvall, WA 98019
(425) 788-1167
www.wildfishconservancy.org

Appendix B
Books

As anglers interested in learning new skills, we have an embarrassment of literary riches available to us, an almost endless shelf of informative how-tos and guidebooks. Indeed, there are almost too many books. How do you filter through the noise to find the best of the best?

The Lyons Press is one of the most venerable publishers of fishing books in America. Over the years, this publisher has given us books on almost every aspect of fishing. You could do far worse than start with the following . . .

Joan Wulff's New Fly-Casting Techniques
Joan Wulff
2012
The first edition of *Joan Wulff's Fly-Casting Techniques* was a classic, and this new edition expands on her techniques, with greater utility to the illustrations. Topics include improving accuracy and distance, loop control, shooting lines, aerial mending, the double haul, correcting common mistakes, and more.

Northern Pike: A Complete Guide to Pike and Pike Fishing
Will Ryan
2005
A good book that examines the habits, habitat, and life cycles of pike as they vary throughout the seasons. The author discusses fishing with bait, lures, and flies, and there is a special chapter on ice fishing.

Pro Tactics: Steelhead & Salmon
W. H. (Chip) Gross
2008
From the Pacific Northwest and Alaska to the Great Lakes, this one covers tackle, baits and lures, and fishing strategies.

Pro Tactics: Walleye
Mark Martin

2008

These tips and techniques for walleye, organized by season, cover topics such as how to trick out your boat, adjusting line length for water depth, using live bait, choosing location, working weed beds, and the author's choices for bait, jigs, and spoons.

The Bass Angler's Almanac: More Than 750 Tips & Tactics (2nd ed.)
John Weiss

2012

The subtitle explains it all: tips and tactics for pursuing bass. This one is very popular (with good reason). Largemouth or smallmouth, lakes and ponds or rivers and creeks, this is the first book a beginning bass angler should buy.

The LL Bean Ultimate Book of Fly Fishing
Macauley Lord, Dick Talleur, and Dave Whitlock

2006

This full-color book for beginning and expert fly anglers alike is divided into four parts—General Fly Fishing, Fly Fishing for Bass, Fly Casting, and Fly Tying—and covers each with in-depth analysis in clear, easy-to-follow language.

The Orvis Fly-Fishing Guide
Tom Rosenbauer

2007

Illustrated by renowned fly-fishing artist Bob White, this guide addresses every significant requirement of fly fishing and provides an excellent founda-tion. Included are instructions for tackle selection; casting and presentation; flies and their specific uses; essential knots and how to tie them properly; successful techniques on stream, pond, or ocean; and information on the best tackle, flies, and methods for pursuing major game fish in fresh and salt water, from bluegill to tarpon.

The Orvis Pocket Guide to Great Lakes Salmon and Steelhead
Matthew Supinski

2004

Starting with descriptions of their food sources, the life cycles of salmon and steelhead, their habits in migration, what they look for in a fly, and when they want it, the author explains the kinds of insects found in the Great Lakes, along with their hatching cycles, and explains variations in flies based on this knowledge. Also provided are tips on how to read the water, with particular emphasis on the peculiarities of the Great Lakes region.

The Orvis Vest Pocket Guide to Leaders, Knots, and Tippets
Tom Rosenbauer
2008
With numerous, easy-to-follow diagrams, this guide offers proper instruction for tying the most useful and effective knots in fly fishing; constructing strong leaders that cast smoothly; understanding knot and tippet breaking strength; and selecting tippets for various fish species and flies, including the newest fluorocarbons.

Index